Pamela Einarsen

Wendy Kann lives in Connecticut with her hus-band and children. This is her first book.

CASTING

WITH A

FRAGILE

THREAD

---

a story of sisters and africa

WENDY KANN

PICADOR

HENRY HOLT AND COMPANY

NEW YORK

www.picadorusa.com

Picador® is a U.S. registered trademark and is used by Henry Holt and Company under license from Pan Books Limited.

For information on Picador Reading Group Guides, as well as ordering, please contact Picador.
Phone: 646-307-5629
Fax: 212-253-9627
E-mail: readinggroupguides@picadorusa.com

Map art © 2006 Laura Hartman Maestro
Book design by Kelly Too

Library of Congress Cataloging-in-Publication Data

Kann, Wendy.
    Casting with a fragile thread : a story of sisters and Africa / Wendy Kann.
        p. cm.
    ISBN-13: 978-0-312-42572-2
    ISBN-10: 0-312-42572-4
    1. Kann, Wendy. 2. Zimbabweans—Connecticut—Biography.
    3. Sisters—Zimbabwe—Biography. 4. Whites—Zimbabwe—Biography.
    5. Zimbabwe—Biography. 6. Connecticut—Biography. I. Title.

CT275.K327A3 2005
968.91'004090092—dc22
[B]

                                                        2005055122

First published in the United States by Henry Holt and Company

First Picador Edition: May 2007

10 9 8 7 6 5 4 3 2

For Lauren

A Noiseless Patient Spider

A noiseless patient spider,
I mark'd where on a little promontory it stood isolated,
Mark'd how to explore the vacant vast surrounding,
    It launch'd forth filament, filament, filament, out of itself,
Ever unreeling them, ever tirelessly speeding them.

And you O my soul where you stand,
Surrounded, detached, in measureless oceans of space,
Ceaselessly musing, venturing, throwing, seeking the
    spheres to connect them,
Till the bridge you will need be form'd, till the ductile
    anchor hold,
Till the gossamer thread you fling catch somewhere,
    O my soul.

—WALT WHITMAN (1819–1892)

contents

Casting with a Fragile Thread

LAUREN

1

Lauren, my youngest sister, was killed in a car accident on a straight and lonely road in Zambia in 1999. By then I was so comfortable in my American life, so warm in its assumptions, that her death felt like a betrayal. Where I live, in Westport, Connecticut, people don't die. Mothers work on the PTA or spend their days, as I do, absorbed in how to improve downtown parking and which plants are deer resistant. On my kitchen table I have a large flat desk calendar and in it I write my three children's play dates and my school, car pool, and social obligations—but I am still notorious for double booking and forgetting things. My friends usually put me at the end of the class phone chain—the system we have for letting people know about snow days and whatnot—because they know it's a little risky to put me in the middle. I make an

...llectually active. I read a lot. Helping my
...neir homework keeps me thinking, and I always
...'R during my long hours in the car to and from
...ivities. My husband fills me in before bed with stories
...   the *New York Times*, if I'm not asleep before he is. By the
time Lauren was killed, it had been years since I had worried
about whether people whom I loved might live or die.

For most of my childhood, death was background noise, like
a TV left on in an empty room. I was born the oldest of three
sisters in 1960 in Salisbury, Rhodesia, a teapot-shaped British
colony in Southern Africa that is now Zimbabwe. When I was
five, the country's two hundred thousand white settlers declared themselves independent from Britain with the Unilateral Declaration of Independence, or UDI, as we called it, in an
effort to guarantee permanent white minority rule. By then,
there had already been alarming changes to the old imperial
world: colonies had crumbled, communism loomed, adults
around me spoke in nervous whispers about Europeans killed
in the African countries to the north of us that had "fallen."
Technically, the Rhodesian civil war began when I was six
and lasted until I was twenty, but initially the African leaders
of the nascent rebel factions (including Robert Mugabe,
Zimbabwe's current president) were disorganized and easily
contained by rigorous emergency legislation imposed after
UDI. By the time I was a teenager, however, the conflict had
spun out of control, leaving Rhodesia embroiled in a bloody
racial clash that lasted until the end of 1979, when warring
parties grudgingly agreed to an uneasy peace through

British-sponsored talks at Lancaster House in London. Robert Mugabe was ultimately voted into office through democratic elections; nationalists renamed the country Zimbabwe. Up to thirty thousand people, black and white, died in the struggle for independence.

Growing up in Rhodesia, there were layers to my experience of death. Not all death was war-related, but it all was part of a more general death hum that seems to hover forever in Africa. There was the drone of faceless names I didn't know. There was the gasp that came with the death of other people's relatives and acquaintances. Then there was the punch that came with the death of those I knew well and loved—my family, my friends.

But at twenty-four, when I arrived in New York, it was as if my childhood had never happened. A path diverted, a faucet of tears turned off. Americans are without a mental image of Zimbabwe, and in its place are only fumbled associations. In Manhattan, when asked who I was I would reply, "I'm Wendy; I'm from Zimbabwe," to which a response of empty eyes would be returned. I began to feel invisible.

It's difficult even for people who live in Africa to see the continent clearly. Our heads are so choked with images of white foreigners adventuring under a romantic sun or haunted black children with distended bellies teetering on skeletal legs that myth tangles itself up with truth like ancient and overgrown wisteria, hiding and distorting what's really there.

But feeling invisible was painful, so I put aside my Zimbabwean identity—like a party dress boxed and wrapped in tissue paper, only to be taken out on special occasions when

I went home—and began to cultivate an American self. For years my new identity felt uncomfortable, like a different dress full of prickles and stays, a corset too tight that sometimes made breathing difficult. Eventually, I stopped looking longingly at the closed Zimbabwean box for something that fitted more easily, as what had initially been painful slowly settled into a dull but manageable throb.

Then Lauren died.

Everyone who dies is remembered by their loved ones as beautiful, but Lauren truly was. She had a particular way of moving that was graceful and deliberate, exuding a sense of, if not serenity, then the feeling that nothing could perturb her. My middle sister, Sharon, who still lives in Zimbabwe, says it was as if Lauren never quite inhabited her body but, instead, seemed to wait lightly outside of herself. Once, when Lauren leaned over to pull a heavy wooden case of beer out from under the bottom shelf on the pantry floor, a huge cobra that had been lurking there reared up and hissed in her face. Richard, her husband, told me she simply wiped her hands on the back of her shorts and went back to the breakfast table, sighing in a ho-hum sort of way. "Richard, there's a cobra in the pantry," she said, while she buttered a piece of toast, as if commenting on the weather.

I can still picture her slow-moving almond-shaped eyes, flawless skin, and high, pronounced cheekbones. She had dark blond hair, which she had highlighted when she lived in Harare, Zimbabwe's capital city, where there are hairdressers, and she used to flick it away from her face with a soft hand in a shy self-conscious manner. Her smile was broad and showed equal amounts of perfectly straight and white upper and lower teeth, which she was proud of and careful to floss.

When Lauren was happy and smiled in that broad way, she was at her most beautiful. When she wasn't happy, which was a lot of the time, she was no less beautiful, but after you first gaped at her you felt her emptiness, a too-long pause that would occur as she floundered in her head, trying to think of what to say. She grew somewhat more certain after she married, but even then those who met Lauren could sense her quiet panic and might grow uneasy and move on, leaving her to drift back into a shadowy periphery, where she was more at home anyway.

She met her husband, Richard, at a party in Wedza, a small and prosperous farming area east of Harare, about ten years after the Rhodesian war ended. It was just like Lauren to drive for three hours alone from Harare on a dark road, on which huge trucks with no headlights rumbled dangerously and abandoned buses waited shrouded in darkness, to go to a party hosted by people she didn't even know. When she called me in New York to tell me about it I muttered maternally at her recklessness and she laughed, explaining that she really needed to meet a new crowd.

Coincidently, Richard didn't know the hosts of the party either. He was from Zambia, an immense country to the north of Zimbabwe that rolls out to almost touch the middle, more unfathomable parts of Africa. There are not many white people in Zambia. Richard, a naturally shy young man then in his late twenties, grew tobacco on the same isolated farm in the southern part of the country where he had grown up.

As Lauren described to me years ago, Richard and two other Zambian bachelors, each still percolating on the warm beer and banter from their daylong drive south, boisterously outdid one another to impress her. But she was most intrigued by Richard. His startling blue eyes were difficult to ignore, his skin was tanned a deep russet, and she felt it still warm from the sun when he draped a self-consciously possessive arm around her shoulders. Fascinated by the romance of isolation, she caught the subtle scent of his loneliness and was touched, in a way, by its intense magnetism.

Lauren and Richard arranged to meet again, a few weeks later, at the elegant Victoria Falls Hotel, on the Zimbabwean side of the Zambian border. Victoria Falls is quite far from Harare, so Lauren flew north. Richard made the long journey south on a potholed ribbon of road in his overheated farm pickup. I remember her telling me how strange their meeting was; Richard's formerly smooth words seemed cut off by the unfamiliar necktie that he had quickly pulled out from the back of a drawer for the occasion, a formal dinner that was regularly interrupted by the noisy clinking of glass and silverware. After coffee Lauren suggested they walk the grounds, and they did, both wondering what to say, the sound of the falls faintly thundering through the far-off trees and the crickets shrieking loud and close.

The hotel pool was bright and deserted, with umbrellas carefully folded and loungers stacked. Lauren laughed unexpectedly and started to unbutton her blouse. She then slipped off her skirt and sandals and stepped out of her underwear. She paused for a long time, quite naked, a little heavier than she liked, her painted toes curled over the edge of the pool, smiling at the water. She let him look at her, young breasts happily unrestrained, tiny goose pimples, shocked and alert, covering her with a fine invisible down. Then she dove in with a small splash, her form cracking and quivering in the illuminated white ripples.

LAUREN WAS WORKING AS A SECRETARY FOR TABEX, THE TO-bacco auction floors in Harare, when she met Richard, a job she felt no qualms about abruptly quitting when I sent her a ticket to visit me in America. I had just had my first baby and spent those long stay-at-home hours lecturing her. I knew Lauren, how much she enjoyed what we in Zimbabwe called a "townie" life: movies and pedicures, cappuccinos (nothing an Italian would recognize), and salads at trendy places for lunch. She had watched a lot of *Dynasty* as a teenager and sometimes still tilted her chin and tried on those upper-crust mannerisms. Once, for a wedding, she rented an enormous feathered hat from Reps Theatre, which she wore with aplomb, blocking views at the church, tickling polite noses in the car, bobbing like a baby ostrich at the luncheon that followed. And she didn't do it as a joke.

I reminded her that even in Zimbabwe, where most farms and their communities were wealthy and established, a farm-ing life was a lonely one in which men and their African labor took on the challenges of the land and left little, really, for their wives to do. Black servants took care of the children and housework. White women kept themselves sane with sewing groups and gardening clubs and flower-arranging circles. They drove trucks long distances, their hairlines full of dust, to visit female neighbors for tea and cake, desperate to confide frustrations with kids or husbands—impatient to forget their isolation, or grumble how hot it was, or wonder aloud, to another white woman, about whether or not it might rain.

I admit I didn't know a lot about Zambia then. In my mind it was one of those limitless slabs of Africa that baked quietly under the relentless sun. Though it had rich copper deposits near its border with Congo and enough fertile land to be plucked up as the British colony they called Northern Rhodesia (Zimbabwe was Southern Rhodesia and then, after Zambian independence, just plain Rhodesia), it never attracted many white settlers. It was too far—well, north, and the malaria was unmanageable, so Britain gave it up fairly easily in the early sixties when nationalists made a fuss.

Many of the girls who boarded at my high school in Salisbury came from Zambia. During the war, Zambia supported freedom-fighter or terrorist camps—it's hard to find the right word for them now—and Rhodesian troops staged dramatic bombing raids on Zambian soil. The thick Zambezi River marks the boundary between the two countries. In those days, the bus that took the Zambian boarders home wasn't allowed to cross the bridge spanning the bottomless gorge where the river becomes the Victoria Falls, so my schoolmates were dropped off in their brown pleated skirts and turquoise blouses and instructed to drag their heavy trunks over steamy concrete and steel into their different and dangerous world.

"Is there at least a club in Choma?" I asked Lauren, on one of those afternoons in Manhattan. Every African farming district I'd ever heard of had a club—a few tennis courts for the ladies or a Sunday afternoon of mixed doubles and a hall-like clubhouse with a long bar at one end. Farmers showered and combed, darkly sunburned, uncomfortably formal in long pants, sipped beer there on Friday or Saturday nights while their wives fussed in the kitchen, swatting flying ants off the beef Stroganoff and pinching moths out of puddings. Parties at rural clubs were notoriously festive, with children sleeping in corners or shrieking on the rickety playground long after midnight. Eventually, somebody's husband would grope another woman or vomit into the flower bed, which gave the district something to gossip about for weeks.

Lauren said that there was a club in Choma, and, during Richard's childhood when Zambia was still Northern Rhodesia, it had once even hosted black-tie dinners, but she laughed now at how hard that was to imagine. The club building still existed, but only just. The swimming pool had been empty for years; its sides collapsing in great concrete lumps atop tufts of grass that pushed through the cracked, chalky bottom. There was a Coke machine—Lauren laughed at my surprise (even Zimbabwean clubs weren't advanced enough for Coke machines)—but then she added that it didn't work. Desperate women sometimes, but not often, drove hot hours to the Choma club to meet other white wives on the potholed tennis court there. It was risky, communication being what it is in Zambia, to plan a game. Too often, one would simply have to sigh and drive those long hours home again after slapping *mopane* flies and mosquitoes, enduring the whimpers of balding kaffir dogs and giggling hellos from scampering bone-thin children practicing their English, who would be intrigued, in a place where nothing changed, by a *mazungu*, or white woman, with a tennis racket.

My motives for dissuading Lauren from Richard were not entirely selfless. I was lonely and wanted her to move to America. During her three months in New York I encouraged her to study, but she chose courses like Off-Broadway Theater, which left her lost in a sea of first-world inside jokes. I encouraged her to date, but one young investment banker I introduced her to spent the evening rudely checking the gold price on something demanding and electronic in his pocket.

Lauren, like me, was baffled by America but had no particular interest in grappling to find an identity that Americans could recognize. We laughed when a young woman on the corner of Sixth Avenue and 49th Street approached us to be part of a TV focus group; when we said we were from Zimbabwe, she said, "I'll just put down New Jersey." Later that same trip, Lauren was spat on by a homeless man on the A train, leaving an oozing oysterlike blob of yellow mucus wandering down the front of her shirt. She left New York in disgust.

LAUREN WAS MARRIED IN THE OLD PRESBYTERIAN CHURCH ON Enterprise Road in Harare and had her wedding reception in the Kariba Room of the Holiday Inn. Richard's Zambian friends packed their best clothes and drove south in pickups and station wagons stuffed with coolers, pillows, and orange peel. Delighted at the excuse for a party, they were nevertheless awkward with the bustle of Harare after their quiet farms. When they arrived, they tapped out quick cigarettes, sucking on them hungrily with uneasy sun-browned lips. Richard's best man, Darren, had long blond hair that fell past his shoulders and wore a string of crocodile teeth on a strip of leather around his neck.

Someone sat my uncle Mark, who was married to my father's sister and had been a cabinet minister during the Rhodesian war, right next to the disco. My uncle Alastair came all the way out from England and gave a speech about Richard, Coeur de Lion—"a colossus straddling the Zambezi"—that nobody understood. Later, when Richard reached far under Lauren's dress to throw her garter, as they do at Zimbabwean weddings, the guys rugby-tackled one another, breaking glasses and knocking over chairs in their eagerness to catch it and show who was who. At the end of the evening Lauren took off her veil and danced alone, swigging champagne out of a bottle, swaying her hips and smiling as she watched her wide wedding skirt swing in mesmerizing circles. She looked up and saw me staring at her. "Wend, let me introduce you," she said, holding my arm and leading me to her new, now more relaxed community, laughing together, intimate and warm. "This is Piers, Murray, Caroline, Penny—" Lauren said, smiling, and in that moment I considered I might have been wrong. Perhaps my hesitations about Zambia had been colored unfairly by the Rhodesian war. It seemed that Lauren might find a little of herself in that mysterious, distant part of Africa, so far away from where I was trying to build a life in New York.

THE CHOMA DISTRICT IN ZAMBIA IS A PLACE WHERE IF THE rains don't wash away the telephone lines, people steal them, since the wire is more useful than the phones (which hardly anyone has). So Lauren and I wrote intermittently and spoke when we could. When we did reach each other, our voices cracking and spitting through the airwaves, our conversations felt broken and unsatisfying, the line usually clicking dead before we had time to say goodbye.

Mostly, we caught up when I visited Zimbabwe. She would make the long drive south and we'd both stay with Sharon and laugh at how different our lives were. She was irritated about the inconvenience of sporadic electricity. She could only use her hair dryer for the few hours they ran the generator at night, which conflicted with preparing dinner. She nearly burned the house down when she hung her robe too close to a candle while taking a shower before dawn, when they started their day.

She complained about long-tailed rats in the toilet and big hairy spiders that came scuttling under the door after the first rains, forcing her to pick up her feet while watching a few precious minutes of generator-run TV. I've seen pictures of her, tagging sportingly along with Richard and his friends on boozy fishing trips, driving hours to particular sandy spots where the Kafue River was most blue. Desperate to protect her beautiful skin from the sun, Lauren spent those weekends

under a tree on the riverbank, her head wrapped
in a sarong—bands of yellow and green swirled over
and under her chin, across her mouth, covering her forehead,
and pulled up over her nose until the soft fabric touched the
two dark rectangles where she had wiggled in her sunglasses
in order to look out onto the river for when Richard came
back on his boat.

She couldn't help but be bored on the farm after the roar
of Richard's motorbike faded into the hot morning and left
nothing to hear except the flies and the soft swish of dry grass
in an occasional breeze. After a while, she chose not to ac-
company her husband on his fishing trips or bird shoots and,
instead, waited alone in her farmhouse for long mind-
numbing weekends. She wanted to plant a lawn, but they
couldn't spare the water. She wanted to make curtains for
their farmhouse, but there was nowhere to buy fabric or
thread.

Meals became an endless and all-consuming chore. Sometimes Richard came home with fish or guinea fowl. Sometimes
she persuaded him to slaughter one of their Brahmin cattle—
peculiar-looking drought- and tick-resistant animals with long
drooping ears and a funny bump between their shoulders.
Every so often lettuce and tomatoes would ripen in the vegetable garden simultaneously and she could make a salad. But
mostly, because she had no experience, she didn't time the
vegetable garden right. For weeks at a time it would yield a
glut of awkward combinations like passion fruit and broccoli
or leeks and strawberries. If she had been bolder with the
other district wives they could have helped, since they had

long ago learned to pool their garden excesses and compromise with shortages. But Lauren didn't talk to them and they, for their part, quickly decided she was snooty.

Every week or so, she took the cooler and drove into Choma. On the way there, children with wobbling, wide enamel basins ran suddenly into the rain-ravaged dirt road to wave limp vegetables; she had to swerve into the bush to avoid them, cursing softly under her breath when thorn bushes squealed sharply against the side of her truck. Once she stopped, but Richard criticized her for it, alarming her with the possibility of contracting cholera from vegetables likely grown too close to sewage. He also warned her not to go into the butcher's in Choma, so she avoided it. Usually the garage on the main Lusaka road opposite the club had bread or chickens. The Super Store almost always had flour, soap, sugar, salt, candles, tea, and an unpredictable assortment of canned goods. On occasion they had a few packets of Zimbabwean pork sausages. There was one time she even found ice cream.

Behind the Super Store was a slow dirt thoroughfare where the buses stopped. An odd tumble of stores built of bare brick and corrugated iron offered warm Coke and thick African beer. A few men calling themselves tailors pedaled Singer sewing machines in a shady place, billowing up dust. There were stalls with noisy vendors hawking toothbrushes and watch parts, who by tomorrow would be selling something different, though it was never what you needed at the time. If you looked behind a swath of plastic sheeting with a faded drawing of a smartly coifed man stapled to it, you'd find a mirror and a stool on which sat a patient barber, swatting flies.

We spent a lot of time in those days discussing the possibility of Lauren's establishing a small business, partly because she and Richard were always short of money, but mostly because she was looking for a reason to be. She tried selling *kapenta*, a teeny dried fish with disconcertingly bulgy eyes that she had to first buy from Lake Kariba, five hours away. The local Africans walked for miles to purchase the fish but, never having more than a few kwacha, they could only afford one cup at a time. Lauren, in her impatient way, was driven up the wall by sacks of smelly fish in her small kitchen and by the streams of Tonga returning with warm, damp banknotes that they'd saved in places close to their skin, all for the profit margin of a penny or two.

Next she tried chickens. She had Richard's laborers build a chicken run near the washing line and then drove all the way up to Lusaka to buy baby chicks. She came home with her precious cargo as carefully as possible although, no matter how mindful she was, a frustrating number of fluffy yellow bodies were lying dead when, at the end of a long day, she opened the big box. Nevertheless, she had me vicariously involved in the complicated regimen of administering vaccines and antibiotics for the survivors, maintaining the chicks at specific temperatures, and fussing with lights, generators, and syringes, which would have her up at all hours of the day and night. Lauren spent weeks smeared with chicken poop and feathers, chasing squawking flapping birds, yelling and shooing at giddy long-tongued dogs, and fiddling with mountains of medication in tiny packets. And yet only a few chickens ever grew to maturity. Those that did had to be slaughtered and plucked, after which Lauren would find bags to put them in, pack the neatly wrapped cadavers in the cooler, and drive them all the way to the Super Store. Though the business didn't last, she was proud that everyone in the district who tasted one of her chickens said they were quite good.

LAUREN SLOWLY LOST THE *OUT OF AFRICA* VISION OF HERSELF that I think had maintained her in the beginning. After a year or two, when I called in the evenings, I heard her softly close the door to the little room they used as an office, shutting out Richard and the drone of cricket on TV, before whispering to me that she was unhappy. She hadn't expected him to be so moody, she said. Sometimes Richard was attentive and loving, helping her plant an herb garden, carrying heavy buckets of precious water and patting down the mud, so she could make the elegant pastas with herb and cream sauce that she had once tried in a fancy Italian restaurant in Harare. (She never did find cream or Parmesan cheese.) Remembering the time when they had torn through the night to get an antimalarial from a far-off farm, she wistfully recalled the concern on his face as he kept glancing at her, huddled in blankets, sweating and shivering on the seat next to him.

But Richard could also be vindictive, even mean. Once, when she had helped herself to a square of chocolate sent to him by his mother, he snatched the rest of the bar up and angrily stormed outside to toss it into the fire that was heating the evening's bathwater. He then refused to speak to her for five lonely days. Silence was his favorite punishment. Sometimes it was hard, she told me, to tell whether the pounding she heard was the rays of the hot sun or her heart beating in the echoing emptiness. Once, at a rare district party, she left the women on the veranda talking about babies and vegetables and sat up at the bar instead, joking and flirting with the men. "It's time to leave," Richard said, appearing sullenly after a short while. But Lauren still had half a gin and tonic to go. Piers and Murray had pulled their bar stools closer to Lauren's and were smiling. She pouted, tilting her head. "Oh, no, can't we stay?"

Richard screeched away that night in a cloud of dust. Much later, Piers and Murray drove Lauren hours out of their way, back to her farm, Semahwa. The little farmhouse waited, crouching in the thick darkness.

"Don't come any closer!" Richard called from the black window, startling them all with his rifle glinting hard in the soft light.

"I think you should leave," Lauren told Richard's friends calmly.

"No . . . ," they stammered, not getting out of the truck. Confused and surely still drunk, they were probably eager to go.

After a short while the taillights of their pickup sucked down to thin pink dots and disappeared with a soft pop. Lauren waited. Africa is not quiet at night. It creaks and groans, settling in on itself, like something eternal that breathes slowly and deep. Dry grass rustled nervously with a million eyes while the wizened watchman, who watched nothing at

Semahwa, least of all the doings of the *wazungu*, the white people, hunched closer over his embers. Lauren sat down on a rock and hummed a little. It didn't seem to matter that her body was cold. Her spirit was very far away.

SO MUCH ABOUT LAUREN CHANGED EVEN BEFORE HER SON WAS born. Her pregnancy seemed to counter her old weightlessness, filling her with a certainty that hadn't been there for a long time. "I'm carrying a boy and his name is Luke," she had told me, long before she ever saw a doctor. When I met him months later at Sharon's house in Harare, Luke was a solid,

Lauren and Luke.

bald baby who seldom cried. Although his eyes were a clear blue, like Richard's, he blinked them in a calm, unhurried way like Lauren. It was a funny coincidence that I had my third child, Sharon her second, and Lauren had Luke all around the same time, and we hooted as we balanced our combined squirmy toddlers into all sorts of cute cousin photos. We would tease Lauren, when Luke remained unperturbed by the ruckus, about how well suited he was to be a Zambian farmer, watching the grass grow. Lauren laughed, but she always seemed a little sensitive to what she imagined Luke's feelings might be and would scoop him up protectively. Once, when we had dozens of visitors over for an afternoon at Sharon's house in Harare, we were feeding the kids the nasty preservative-and-nitrite-stuffed red frankfurters that all Zimbabwean children love, when Lauren came out of the kitchen, primly, with a little bowl of steamed vegetables—only enough for her darling baby son.

SIX MONTHS AFTER THAT VISIT TO ZIMBABWE, IT WAS A SATURDAY in Westport. Mickey, the kids, and I had just come back from a weekend away, sunburned and insect-repellent sticky. Outside, the air had that salty-fish taste of Long Island Sound, while inside it was thick and stale from too-long-shut windows. When I heard Sharon on the answering machine, I knew the slippery pregnancy she had been holding on to for weeks was lost. I was surprised, however, when I called her and Lauren answered the phone. "Hi, Wend," she said in her calm, knowing way. I was relieved to find her there. She had driven the ten hours from her farm with Luke and Luke's nanny, Lucy, and we whispered about Sharon and her sorrow and all the support she was going to need. Lauren was lucky to have Lucy, I said, especially at a time like this. I knew Lauren had brought many women in from the tobacco fields or grading sheds to help her after Luke was born, but she had usually sent them back after a day or two. Lucy, Lauren had told me months before, was intelligent and learned quickly. Luke loved her, Lauren assured me now.

I called regularly, endlessly talking to Sharon about blood and babies and amniotic fluid. After a few days, Laurern answered the phone again. "I haven't asked how you are, Lol," I remembered.

"Did I tell you about the geraniums?" she replied thoughtfully.

"No."

"Well, I heard that in the south of France they grow scented geraniums, which they press to extract essential oils," she explained. "Geraniums also grow beautifully in the dry Zambian climate," she went on.

We never got to the part about where she would find or pay for the special kind of press or the little bottles she would need to put the oil in or how she would distribute it. But I liked the idea a whole lot better than chickens or smelly dried fish. I could picture Lauren inspecting her acres of scented geraniums, perhaps a little absentmindedly, with her slow-moving almond-shaped eyes. I could easily imagine the dusty fly-beleaguered farmhouse she'd described giving off the faint but pleasing aroma of geranium-scented oil.

. . .

A WEEK AFTER SHARON'S MISCARRIAGE THE PHONE RANG IN the very early morning, startling me awake, then abruptly stopping, prompting a brief expectant pause followed by a loud wail from the other room. Irritated, I remembered that Sunday was *my* day to get up with the baby. Mickey grunted and rolled over, pulling the pillow over his head. I shuffled to where Samantha was crying, pink-cheeked and disoriented in her crib, and while I lifted her little body out the phone rang again. I hurried to answer it, gritty sarcasm ready.

"Wendy?" It was Sharon's husband, Butch.

"Oh, hi, Butch," I said, wondering why, after fifteen years, my African relatives still didn't understand time zones.

"I've got some bad news for you," he said.

How bad could it be? I'd spoken to Sharon a dozen times in the past week. She was still shaky, but seemed to be recovering.

Butch hesitated slightly before he said the words. "Lauren's dead."

I must have made some kind of noise because suddenly Mickey was there, taking Samantha from me. Doubled over, I couldn't hold on to her. What do you say when your sister has died, *Where? How?* Words felt too light, too conversational. Butch continued to speak heavily, explaining that Lauren had died on the drive back from Harare to the farm. He understood Luke might be alive. He and Sharon were leaving for Zambia immediately. Richard knew nothing more. He had cried on the phone, Butch said, and had begged, "Please come," and "I can't cope."

The details would remain unknown for a long time. In Zambia, people communicate over two-way radios that crackle and skip, making it difficult to hear. That Sunday morning while we were still asleep in Connecticut a tangle of messages with burning electric edges and no resolution was carried on the waves. Anyone listening within a hundred-mile radius of Richard's farm knew there had been an accident involving a name that sounded like Duckett, Lauren's married name, but it could have been Beckett. Everyone was alert, unsure. A farmer close to the crash raced to investigate. So did the local veterinarian. Piers and Murray, Richard's friends, each many miles away in opposite directions, drove wildly to get to him.

Cruelly, Richard was oblivious a little longer. He was distracted and getting the house ready, ignoring the radio muttering to itself quietly in the small farm office. He was happy and excited that Lauren and Luke were coming home, eager for light chatter and warm bodies to ease the crushing loneliness of the bush.

It's hard to know what alerted him. A brittle word maybe, just caught, drifting into his awareness like a leaf. Somewhere in his pottering Richard became conscious of urgent voices; then something frozen expanded in his chest. His nervous fingers dialed Penny, a neighbor, who helplessly overflowed with what she knew. Richard stumbled outside, disbelieving, just as Piers and Murray arrived, scrambling from their vehicles and quickly slamming heavy truck doors. "What's going on?" Richard shouted, as they strode toward him, but still no one knew for sure, and the three of them stood paralyzed for long minutes in the dust and sun while the radios in their pickups crackled on callously and finally spat out a name. Duckett. It was definitely Duckett.

2

There is a place you go when someone you love dies, a hyper-reality where you hear your own breath, where other people are moving slowly and talking loudly. Your tongue feels thick, colors are brighter, and things zoom into focus too close to your face and surprise you. I had been there before, so I thought I knew the landscape. But when Butch called and I heard the words "Lauren's dead," it was as though I had disappeared completely. Rage and fear were all that was left, quivering and rippling where my body used to be.

As I ran from my front door the morning I left Westport for Lauren's funeral, Mickey shouted after me. He was standing in the doorway of our clapboard house, our children clutching tight fistfuls of his pajamas. Sebastian was seven by then, Claudia was four, and Samantha was eighteen months.

Sugar maple trees rippled a languorous silver-green. The fat tang of a freshly cut lawn hung in the air. "What do I feed them?" he yelled.

"There are lots of chicken nuggets in the freezer," I shouted back, shaking off my American life as I climbed into the cab.

I flew to Victoria Falls in Zimbabwe, cocooned in a humming aircraft for a night and a day. I listlessly watched a movie, tossed in fitful sleep, scribbled down words that felt like Lauren, panicking that her essence was already slipping from me. When I was exhausted, I closed my eyes and tried to touch the parameters of the place I found myself in, but I couldn't feel the edges.

Sharon and Butch were waiting at the airport to take me across the Zambian border for the three-and-a-half-hour drive to the farm. Sharon's eyes were puffy and red-rimmed. She insisted, pressing her lips together to stop their trembling, that her miscarriage was forgotten and unimportant, even though it was hardly more than a few days old.

As we crossed baking asphalt to their pickup, Sharon told me she had already been up to the farm and that Luke, who was seventeen months old, was apparently uninjured except for cuts and scrapes. A veterinarian had examined him. "A *vet?*" I asked.

"It's Zambia," Sharon said, going on to explain that the X-ray machine at the clinic was broken. Luke had spent the night "under observation" in Mazabuka, sleeping incongruously between the vet and his wife, warm, I imagine, in their unfamiliar intimacy. The same vet was also going to conduct the funeral service.

"What about the nanny?" I asked.

"Lucy's in the clinic in Mazabuka. Her family has to take her food because clinics here are too poor to feed their patients," she said, scribbling something down. "And they used Lucy's only blanket for Lauren's body so we need to buy her another one," she remembered, writing again. I thought about Lauren's pale body in a coarse African blanket sticky with blood as I felt my skin slide on the hot vinyl of the pickup seats. Dully efficient, Sharon checked her notes, unaware that I couldn't understand anyway, that my mind hadn't caught up. She listed who was already at the farm, who still had to arrive, and how they would get there. She thought we should sing "Fill the World with Love," the song from *Goodbye, Mr. Chips* that Sharon had sung at Lauren's wedding. She mentioned a eulogy and I nodded in assent, briefly wondering how people make themselves intelligible through devastation, abstractly curious if there might be a trick or a code I could learn. Dry African air, heavy with dust and wood smoke, rushed at our faces through the open windows, one childhood smell after another. My sister and I felt a sanctuary, a reprieve in the weight of her broad diary on our laps, watching the smooth blue ink flow out of her pen.

We had a shopping list. Zambians she had met on the farm the day before had told Sharon that Spar, on the Zimbabwean side of the border, was the best place to stock up on food and alcohol. We pulled into a gritty parking lot that smelled of heat and burnt rubber. People milled with baskets of fruit, sacks of cornmeal on their shoulders, dry loaves of bread poking out of thin plastic bags. Women sat straight-legged on blankets holding bright umbrellas as they arranged tomatoes or oranges in rows and pyramids or braided one another's hair. Men huddled in the sliver of shade at the entrance to the store, loudly meting out kerosene or cooking oil into grubby containers. Somewhere, a small transistor radio turned on full volume hissed and twanged with scratchy African music. Dusty goats chewed idly on thorns, and skeletal curved-back dogs snapped hopefully at air. Butch staggered into the small store with clinking wooden cases filled with empty beer and Coke bottles for exchange while Sharon and I waited in the truck. "Maybe I should take Luke back to America with me," I blurted, when we were alone. My words hung awkwardly in the stifling heat, embarrassing me.

"I wouldn't mention anything to Richard just yet," Sharon finally said. "Let's see how things go."

We cleared Zimbabwean customs, and as we crossed the bridge over the falls I peered at the white waters churning so far down in the bottom of the gorge. I noticed that there were more prowling baboons at the Zambian border post than there had been at the Zimbabwean one, and they foraged for food around parked vehicles, the big males curling their lips threateningly at people who honked or threw stones at them. We drove through Livingstone, the Zambian border town. Old colonial arches and verandas were painted in faded African colors, and there were scrawled signs offering safaris or river cruises. A half hour out of Livingstone we were stopped at a roadblock where we answered questions with cautious mono-syllables and smiled ingratiatingly while a policeman peered suspiciously from under his cap, fingering his gun, before im-patiently waving us on.

We were only truly on our way then: miles and miles of shimmering gray road peeling out emptily north into the heat. A few times I asked Sharon, "Is that Choma?" squinting hopefully into the distance, and she shook her head, taking off her sunglasses to wipe the sweat from her eyes on her T-shirt sleeve.

I'd never visited Lauren before, for reasons that went be-yond the one I'd given her: that my children might get malaria. Sharon had driven all the way to Semahwa only once, a year or so after Lauren was married. "I wouldn't bother," she had warned me quietly then. "It's boring. There's no pool and no one to visit. There's not even a security fence."

We continued driving. The sun drummed numbingly. End-less dry bush reached far into the horizon on either side of us. Occasionally we sped through a far-flung lonely settlement: a gas station, a store, a dusty tumble of accommodations made from brick and corrugated iron. Ragged children ran out to wave or to shout drowned English words at our vehicle as we passed.

"There it is." At last Sharon pointed ahead to a town only faintly more substantial than the settlements we'd passed, and when we got there we turned off and bumped into the bush, following dirt tracks. "It's less than an hour now," Butch said jerking over rutted sand, as we hurriedly wound up our windows to shut out the dust. He drove very slowly on the

narrow ruined road to avoid rocks and gullies while also being careful of the bicycles, goats and ox-drawn carts that
seemed to appear from nowhere, startling us.

It was late afternoon by the time we reached the farm. We
drove through the compound where the farm laborers lived,
scattering children and chickens in our wake. Tall tobacco
barns, which I knew housed racks of curing leaves, curled thin
plumes of smoke above their flat tin roofs. We passed a grading shed, a water reservoir, a workshop, a few mud-splashed,
formerly whitewashed rooms where Richard's most important workers, like his foreman and mechanic, lived. Farther
off in the bush, on the right, was an untidy clearing where
a dozen or so round thatched huts were half hidden by a
falling-down grass fence. Indistinct as shadows, people starting their evening fires glanced up as our truck turned onto the
long dirt road that ran from the compound to the main house.

Sharon, like a tired tour guide, pointed out the spindly flam-
boyants that Lauren had planted on either side of the road,
trees that decades from now would be majestic and arching
but were then only a reminder that the farm was weak and
struggling. At the split-pole gate where the small dry lawn suddenly started there was a hand-painted sign that read DRIVE
SLOWLY! CHILDREN AND PUPPIES AT PLAY! I also noticed the
gum-pole window boxes, the exuberant ivy, and the tropical
plants Lauren had slowly cultivated. I registered the lavish
magenta bougainvillea draping the small whitewashed water
tower and garage.

Richard came out of the kitchen carrying Luke, letting the
torn screen door slam behind him. He muttered "Thank you

for coming so quickly" to the dry lawn at his feet before giving me a clumsy hug. Luke squirmed in Richard's arms, bewildered and fractious while we all stood there outside the kitchen for a little while, caught in the smoke from the crackling fire under the water tank, enveloped in our common sorrow. I reached out, tentatively, to touch the deep gash on Luke's ankle, and he cried out loudly, clambering up his father's body like a cat. "Lucky," I whispered, not really meaning it.

"I'm glad it's still light," Richard said, still not looking at me, uncomfortable with the sudden intimacy. "We've been waiting for you to find a place for the grave." I moved to get my bags and take them inside, but he said, "We need to go now. It gets dark soon, and we have to start digging early to-morrow because the ground is dry and hard."

Me. The oldest sister with the strong opinions and answers, the one who brings back cutting-edge American ideas—he thought I would know where to bury Lauren. We walked silently with Sharon, the slipping sun spilling orange and pink, the dirt and stones of the long compound road crunch-ing under our feet. "Was there a particular place Lauren liked to walk?" I asked, politely almost, still not thinking clearly. Richard shrugged and we resumed our aimless silence for a while longer. He must remember the places on the farm she had thought were beautiful, for Christ's sake. "Well, where's the dam?" I asked, impatient. She had once told me she used to walk around the dam.

"It's too far away," Richard said. "I think she should be closer. Like here." He pointed, showing us. We were on the compound road about three hundred yards from the house.

"Or here." He waved his hand at the other side of the road, which appeared to be exactly the same. Sharon and I looked at each other. We wanted a beautiful place with deep water, a glade or a shrine—a place that reflected Lauren's soul. Richard was waving at bush. We tilted our heads and squinted at each side, trying to see beyond the bush, fighting back tears, not wanting to do this. I turned to one side and strode deep into the long grass looking for something, anything. I finally found a tall forked msasa tree with two smaller msasas and a spindly acacia close by. If you ignored the scrub and thorns, together they made a circle, a canopy, something like a glade.

"What about this?" I indicated the spot with my arms. "We can clear this scrub and dig her grave here." I felt light-headed and paused a moment. "We can cut a wide path from the road. . . ." I stopped again, thinking I was going to be sick. "The hearse will have to get quite close," I said quietly, meaning it as a question, not wanting an answer.

I inhaled deeply and tried to force the choking out of my chest. My entire body tingled and I felt myself floating. I closed my eyes, and when I opened them again Richard and Sharon were watching me. "This msasa is so beautiful," I said, exhaling, tipping my head back to drain away tears. I stared at the imposing flat-topped tree above us. The sky behind it was turning a deep blue-black. I remembered how low stars hang in Africa. You felt they were too hot and waited for them to make some sort of sound.

"You'll have to start at five a.m. tomorrow," Richard said. It was clear he didn't want any part of this. "I'll get some guys to help you." We walked back to the house in the dark.

. . .

When the screen door slammed behind me I found myself in Lauren's kitchen. I stood there for a while, not moving the air, trying to hold on to her. I looked around. The Formica on the narrow kitchen counter had been burned and showed sores of splintery wood. A bare lightbulb dangled weakly. My feet were on the floor she had covered in the Martha Stewart black-and-white checkerboard pattern I had sent her only a few months before, which was already peeling. I touched things gently with my fingertips: her small stove, her complicated list for rotating vegetables in the garden. If I breathed slowly and shallowly, I believed I might not loosen her spirit. I smiled at familiar posters on the wall and odd pieces of my grandmother's china in the pantry. I walked slowly down her wide hall, noticing a too-narrow blue runner lying at an odd angle on the invariable red polished concrete of an African farmhouse. The walls were lined with pictures, mostly of our relatives; in the collage she had made of her wedding photographs, snapshots were slipping to the bottom of the frame.

Sharon called me, and I followed her voice to the right of the T shape the hall made and into Lauren and Richard's bedroom, where dozens of Lauren's brightly colored scrunchies were shoved onto all four bedposts, like a Mexican fiesta, and we giggled together with a kind of giddy relief: "Typical." A robe behind the door, when we pushed our faces into it, still held her scent. Hairbrushes, perfume, and crumbling eye shadow lay on her vanity table. Old *Cosmopolitan* and *Fair Lady* magazines were piled high next to her bed, and bossy notes in her handwriting were taped to the bathroom door, dictating how to flush the toilet with strong reminders to put the seat down.

Sharon and I walked to the other end of the hall, passing big storage cupboards, strangely content as though we were all together again, visiting Lauren at last. The small office had a desk and farm radio and shelves of neatly stacked files. Pictures of our children and us were blue-tacked to the wall along with yellowing inspirational poems. An old manual typewriter was covered with a tea towel and pushed into the corner of the desk. An unmailed letter to me lay stamped on top of it.

"I received your parcel for Luke on Wednesday." I heard her voice so clearly as I read aloud. "I can't wait to see you in Harare for Christmas," Lauren wrote—*I can't wait to see you in Harare for Christmas, I can't wait to see you in Harare for Christmas*—and then I couldn't see her words on the page anymore, and no sound came from my throat, and Sharon and I held each other, shuddering as she grew fainter, and I reached out with my heart, fighting to cling to her, trying to forget I'd already seen her accidental shrine.

UNABLE TO SLEEP, A LITTLE AFTER MIDNIGHT I HEARD LUKE running down the hall, disoriented and confused, shrieking, "Mama, Mama!" I stumbled through the dark to get to him quickly, and he scratched and cried in my arms until Richard emerged groggily to gather him up. They disappeared together, Luke still whimpering, the light from Richard's bedroom snuffing out softly as he closed the door.

I lay there in the dark fighting memories and regret for hours longer and then, when the day was close, woke Sharon. We went out into the chilly morning to find the men Richard had mentioned the night before. They were squatting, warming themselves around a small fire and sucking at thick wedges of tobacco rolled up in newspaper. When Sharon and I approached, they stood up, shifted their eyes, and moved their calloused feet in the dust, dangling their tools bound by strips of bark and bits of old tire, waiting passively for instructions.

I motioned that they follow us to the place we had chosen and then said, as loudly as I could, as if shouting to people on the other side of a too-wide gulf, "I want you to dig a very deep hole." I scanned their faces for a glimmer of understanding. One man nodded and picked up a stick, indicating that he wanted me to mark the corners of the grave.

How big do you dig your sister's grave? It sounded like a little girls' clapping game or skipping song. I looked at Sharon, who snapped into efficient mode. "Well," she said tentatively, "Lauren was five foot five. But then again, Butch did say they only had the very big coffins in stock in Lusaka. . . ." Ah, another line to the song: *"How big do you dig your sister's grave, and what do you do if the coffin doesn't fit?"*

Sharon and I wandered back and forth from the house to monitor the slow progress of the grave, hypnotized by what appeared to be its endless depth, curiously revived by our own orders to the passive and silent workers: "Take down that sapling—cut that grass—trim that tree—make a path." We rummaged in Lauren's closet for something to bury her in and chose the expensive clothes she had bought in South Africa for special occasions: pretty underwear, a pressed white blouse, and light-gray wool Daniel Hector pants. We knew we weren't going to open her coffin at the funeral—Butch had told us, when he identified her body, that her face was badly bruised—but it was August, winter in Zambia, and even though she was dead we wanted her to be warm.

The house began to fill with people who were arriving from great distances to attend the funeral. I heard Richard on the radio telling the pilot of a light aircraft from Harare that, yes, there was a grass landing strip; no, he was not sure when it was last checked; no, the pilot should not buzz it because that would bring out all the villagers and they'd crowd, gaping, and make landing impossible. Neighbors tiptoed carefully in and out of our grief, carrying casseroles and extra mattresses, laying out bedding in the living room and in the hall. Butch, sensitive about his tremendous snoring, volunteered to sleep in the kitchen with Chunky, the old Rottweiler, and half a dozen Jack Russells, all of whom were delighted with the company.

Hundreds of flowers began to appear in grubby plastic buckets and old kerosene cans. Most district families had lavish gardens; some even grew roses as a crop. Some flowers came from people who didn't know Lauren or have any intention of coming to the funeral. Richard's friends milled, waiting to help. Sharon and I felt like hostesses at a party where the guests were bored, so we had them tie bouquet after bouquet, which we arranged extravagantly in the area the laborers had cleared. I considered, whimsically, to no one in particular, how nice it might be to have flowers in the trees, and moments later Murray and Piers, in a pickup full of Richard's friends, came revving through the long grass with tall ladders and hammers, willing to climb whatever tree I so much as nodded at.

The hearse arrived late from Lusaka. By then the hole in the ground was well over the heads of the two shirtless black men who were still inside it, scraping at the stubborn, compact earth.

I was irritated that Lauren's coffin was dusty and ran to find a rag in the kitchen, coming back to clean it carefully, knowing the casket was too big, trying to imagine where her hair and fingers were in its dull expanse, searching out where to caress them.

Moments before three o'clock, when the ceremony was scheduled to begin, Sharon and I begged Richard to look at the grave, which he had doggedly avoided until then, to help him steel himself before the funeral. And so, wearing the dark suit he was married in and carrying Luke, Richard went with Sharon and me, each of us walking alone along the compound road. Sharon and I were proud of how we had transformed the bush, showing him the wide path we'd cut and the flowers we'd strewn. Someone had opened folding chairs and set them out in an orderly way in the uneven slashed-down grass.

Richard stood holding Luke in the dappled shade of the tall msasa, next to that seemingly bottomless hole in the red earth. He scuffed his leather shoes in the expanse of sand where the saplings and thornbushes used to be. His eyes shifted, disbelieving, over the enormous dull-brown coffin waiting there under the acacia on a special stand. A breeze tugged slightly, stirring dust and the faintly rotting scent of warm roses nailed to trees. Luke whined a little and arched his back, squirming to get down. Leaves fluttered silver and dusty pink. Cicadas screeched. The Jack Russells that had followed us yapped and chased lizards, rustling the brush on a nearby dry anthill. No one knew what to say.

ON SOME SUBTLE CUE, THEY CAME SLOWLY: A MASS OF PEOPLE walking down the compound road and quietly flowing onto our wide-cut path. Too-tanned women in their slightly dated frocks and worn heels, men in ill-fitting suits and floppy farmer's hats, which they took off when they got closer, folding them discreetly into their hands. Lauren's old townie friends struggled in their strappy sandals, mismatched borrowed sweaters, and narrow fashionable skirts from Johannesburg.

Africans walked from the other direction, in flimsy fragments of brown and gray, teenagers turning for reassurance from the adults behind them, jostling and bumping, giggling nervously, making their procession jerky and unsure. They had offered to sing for us. We had offered to pay them. They stood a little distance off and to one side of our ceremony, waiting for their prompt.

Ian Parsons, the vet, read Psalm 23 and spoke graciously about "still waters running deep" and Lauren's lovely smile. Lauren's good friends, Penny from Choma and Sherie from Harare, both read poems and talked about old times, weeping as they recalled how much they'd miss her. I gave my eulogy buoyed by an odd energy that let me see myself from afar.

I wore a black and gray wide-collared sweater that had slipped slightly at the neck, revealing a little of my bra strap. Red dust colored my shoes and the hem of my pants. As the sun beat through the barely stirring leaves, sweat glistened slightly on the bridge of my nose. I spoke clearly and expressed myself so animatedly that Ian Parsons had to put his hand up protectively when I stepped alarmingly close to the edge of the grave.

My faraway self looked at the people watching me, shocked there were so many of them—far too many for the folding chairs in the rough-hewn grass—all of them listening to me intently from their clusters in the sun, fanning themselves with copies of "To Fill the World with Love." Some were sniffing quietly. Even the ruddy-faced men, who had tackled one another at Lauren and Richard's wedding, were blinking back tears. Johann, a tall hunter intimidating even by Zambian standards, was weeping openly. Suddenly, I was filled with a deep and debilitating sadness that Lauren wasn't there to witness how she was mourned, and only then did I hear my voice crack and see myself cry. Luckily, I was almost at the end of what I had to say and as I returned to my seat I felt people pat me on the back and murmur, "Well done."

Murray, Piers, Darren (Richard's best man), and Johann lowered the casket, winding it down slowly on special pulleys. When they had finished, Richard picked a red rose from a bucket and carried Luke closer to the grave. Luke anxiously scanned the solemn faces staring back at him, searching, it seemed, for his mother. Uncomfortable with the attention and impatient with his own sorrow, Richard gave Luke the flower, then just as quickly shook it out of the confused toddler's chubby fist. The rose seemed to tumble down, down, down, until it hit on Lauren's too-big coffin with a hollow thud. At Ian Parson's nod, the people from the compound began their song, a haunting a cappella that wound and soared in such clear and mournful notes that as I stood there, listening, it was as if their sound came from within me rather than without. The sun, which is very big in Africa, was dropping in the late-afternoon sky. A slight breeze picked up, and people sighed and pushed their hair back and shook their faces into it, drying off their sweat and tears. Then we walked slowly back to the house. The singers from the compound followed us at a respectful distance, expecting a meal, which is traditional at African funerals, but instead Murray gave them money—a bundle of dirty kwacha notes—and shooed them away at the gate. The rest of us mingled on Lauren's dry patch of lawn, picked the flies out of the milk, and had tea and cake, followed by heavy and solemn drinking.

Sharon and I stayed with Richard for a few days after the funeral. He fumbled with the cloth diapers we taught him how to fold. We showed him the cream for diaper rash and the ointment for conjunctivitis, and we reminded him to cut Luke's nails and wash his hair. We pointed out the educational books and toys Lauren had so painstakingly collected, and I lectured him about child development. We suggested that he sleep with Luke; it would be company for them both. When Richard was out of sight, Sharon and I whispered to each other, concerned about the way he stared off into the distance, worried about who would cook, if either of them would eat, if he could cope.

"I can always . . . ," I looked at Richard and let my words tail off gently.

"Luke is all I have," he retorted, a sudden hardness flashing in his eyes.

So Sharon and I urgently discussed child care while Richard stared listlessly at the horizon. When and even *if* Lucy came back, it seemed certain she could never manage without Lauren. Besides, I argued, we needed someone who could read. Luke really should know stories like *The Three Little Pigs* and *Goldilocks*. Maybe we could find a pensioner from Zimbabwe or a young girl just graduated from college who wants to see the world? Someone's relative could easily put up a notice in a church or supermarket in England; I thought about the Y, in Westport. Surely any young woman would love an opportunity to go to Africa? We spread our marmalade a little doubtfully.

Shortly before we were due to return home, rumors from the compound drifted in that Lucy was arriving from the hospital on the next bus. Desperately relieved, we crowded into the front of Richard's old farm pickup, not the reliable uninsured one that Lauren had died in but the one with the holes in the floorboard and the badly cracked windshield. I sat with Luke on my lap, holding him protectively, anxious that he should see a familiar face, hoping it might comfort him. The bus stop was in Choma behind the Super Store. We waited there as two or three noisy, exhaust-rattling diesel buses disgorged themselves before, finally, Richard said, "There she is."

A tall slim woman, graceful in her obvious pain, climbed slowly out of the bus amid bundled belongings hurled down from its dusty roof. The side of her face was crisscrossed with dozens of angry stitches marching and invading her nostrils, her earlobes, and the corners of her eye, each glinting blue and black. Sharon climbed into the flatbed of the pickup, starkly white and resolute against the many other people who had already noisily accumulated there. "Wait," Richard began, uneasy with the thought of broaching conventional boundaries and protocol, but Sharon ignored him. Lucy sat next to me on the plastic seat in the cab, whimpering at every gully and fissure. Rather than being comforted, Luke appeared horrified and startled by the stranger beside him.

Lucy didn't want to go straight home. She wanted to see Lauren's grave, so Sharon and I walked her there from the compound end of the road, taking a shortcut through the dry grass, supporting her on either side. The grave was piled high with pink soil, the packed dirt not nearly fitting back into the cavernous hole from which it had been taken. Richard's friends, who had shoveled the loose dirt back themselves, had

Lucy.

also gathered up the bouquets and piled them, bountiful and tumbling, on top of that little mountain, and they lay there still, limp and wilting, marking where she was. Before we got very close, Lucy stopped and exhaled a long and ragged breath.

We held tightly to Lucy's arms, sensing her body was weak, waiting to move at her nod, but she stood there, staring at Lauren's grave from a distance. She started to speak softly about the accident. They were driving on a long straight road, she said, the kind where the asphalt has been slathered on thickly, like the frosting on a cake, with a deep step down to the earth on both sides. Luke was sleeping on her lap in the backseat when she heard Lauren give a little gasp as one wheel slipped off the asphalt and onto the gravel below. Lauren turned the wheel sharply to right the car, but she was traveling fast, so the pickup veered all the way over to the opposite side of the road, forcing her to overcorrect again. Lucy described a light-headed pause, a momentary loss of traction with the road, and the weightless horror of unrestrained steel and rubber spinning over asphalt, and in that sliver of a second she had covered Luke's body with hers, never hearing the thunder of metal and glass as the vehicle crashed and tumbled wildly against the hard and unforgiving earth.

"When I wake up," Lucy said, shaking her head softly at the memory, "Luke is screaming very, very loud. The car is upside down. The wheels are still going around and around and around." She paused and squeezed her eyes tightly together. "Luke is standing in the middle of the road, so I pick him up, and I go to find the madam." She paused again and looked down, squeezing my hand tightly as though she wanted to brace herself against pain. Sharon and I listened closely as air passed through her lips. "The madam is too far on the other side of the car. Her face is in the stones next to the road," Lucy said. "There is too much blood—here." Lucy touched her own temple and shook her head. "She is alive, but maybe just a little bit," Lucy went on quietly.

"Maybe ten minutes I am waiting," Lucy said. "There is too much blood in my face, and I cannot see. Luke, he is still crying too loud. It is very hot." Lucy shifted her feet in the sand, as if trying to plant them more firmly. "Your sister has so little breathing," Lucy said. The wind made our faces sting cold. The day was sighing into night.

"Then a bwana, a white man, is stopping. A madam is running and running from their car but your sister"—Lucy paused—"but your sister is now dead." We stood in silence, my skin no longer protecting me, and I felt like part of the evening, indistinguishable from it.

"The bwana is radioing the police, but first he is taking your sister's rings and watch for you," Lucy said. "The police they are taking me to the hospital."

"I'm sorry," Lucy said.

The three of us held on to one another in the grass, still a distance from Lauren's grave, and we wept, tears snagging on Lucy's stitches. When there were no more tears and it was practically dark, we slowly walked Lucy back to the compound, past glowing fires boiling evening water in old paraffin tins, small children giggling in clutches, chickens clucking from their twiggy coops built high off the ground with knotty branches. On reaching the door of Lucy's small round hut, she stumbled a little at the single step so I grabbed her elbow while Sharon pushed open the tin door. It smelled of smoke and carbolic soap. Lucy walked across the dirt floor to a neat dresser and fumbled for a box of matches, which she struck and then drew the cupped flame to half of a candle melted onto an enamel saucer.

"Your room is nice, Lucy," I said, foolishly.

"It leaks," she replied.

Light flickered in the one cracked mirror. A string was nailed across one side of the room and two dresses hung on it. An angular metal bed was half hidden behind a worn curtain. "Do you need help?" we asked, uncertain in Lucy's space; she hesitated, so we walked her the few extra steps to her bed, held aside the curtain, and she lay down stiffly there and closed her eyes. I looked about for a covering but then remembered her blanket. "Sharon and 1 will get you another blanket tomorrow," I said quickly, and she closed her eyes and nodded. "Good night, Lucy," I said, not knowing what else to add, drawing the curtain a little and then stepping away, pulling her door shut behind us.

I had lived in Africa for twenty-four years, but this was the first time I had felt intimacy with a black person.

CHILDHOOD

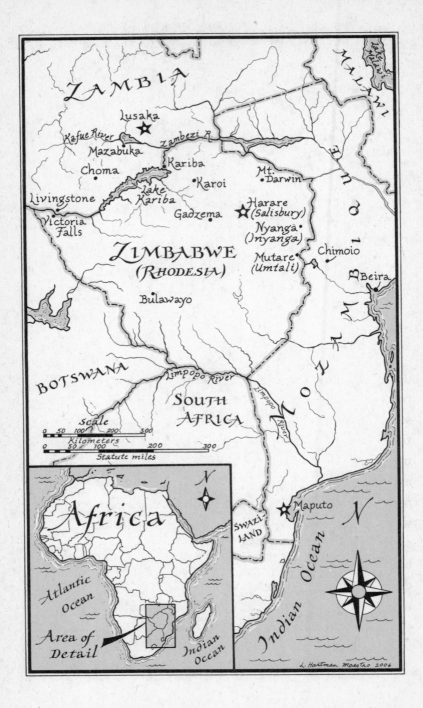

L. Hartman Maestro 2006

3

In 1965 I climbed onto a chair to look into the mirror of my mother's kidney-shaped dressing table. Serious brown eyes stared back at me. Sharon sucked her thumb close by, her three-year-old body naked and tanned butter-brown. I picked up the heavy sewing scissors, angled them against my scalp, and snipped off a large handful of my long hair, while Sharon regarded me critically in the mirror, her own towhead still short and baby-fine. I realigned the scissors with my eyebrows and lopped off another bit of hair from the other side. We both frowned at my new image: almost-blond hair straight down my back, uneven brown tufts at my temples. Sharon said nothing, probably imagining, even then, that I, the older sister, knew exactly what to do next. I considered the possibility of trying to stick my hair back on and glanced around my parents' bedroom, which still smelled like Cobra Floor Polish and Handy Andy from Margaret's cleaning it that morning. A big rain spider scuttled across the pale wall.

Beyond the white curlicue burglar bars in the windows came the scent of our Salisbury suburb—wood smoke, sweet gardenia, and recently watered earth drying quickly under a hot sun. Sparrows squabbled in the eaves of our flat roof. I could hear Margaret, who had gone to get herself an enamel cup of sweet milky tea, and who always spoke more loudly when my mother wasn't home, clicking and clucking in Shona with both Josiah, who was yelling from the kitchen, and Isaac, who was yelling from the yard. Sharon still studied my reflection. "Your hair lookth funny," she lisped at last, solemn flat words squeezing around her thumb. It was true. It looked terrible. But I imagined I could tidy myself up a bit, so using both hands I aimed the huge scissors at the rest of my hair and began to hack.

"*Eee weh!*" Margaret screamed, running forward to snatch the scissors out of my hands. Josiah appeared a few moments behind her, wiping his forearms on his apron, stopping suddenly when he saw me. "*Eeh, eeh,* sorry," he said, shaking his head and chuckling softly at my bald patches and bristles and the scraggly Davy Crockett tail down my back.

Margaret did not think it was so funny. "You will get a smack!" she shouted angrily at me, the white maid's cap my mother had bought her from the OK Bazaars wobbling furiously on her tight braids as she swept my soft fallen hair quickly with her hands.

I tried to imagine what my mother, who was unlikely to hit me, would really do when she saw me. Possibly, she would weep. Maybe she would run thoughtful fingers through the stubble and try to fix it. Most likely, she would stand barefoot and supple-limbed, towering above me, throwing back her dark hair and laughing in her special way that rang in my ears and made strangers want to move closer to her.

Sometimes, my mother made me feel a little like the nuns who wondered how-do-you-solve-a-problem-like-Maria in *The Sound of Music*, which we had watched together at the Royal Cinema. Although once, when she took Sharon and me to see two teenage lions that had been chained, for some un- fathomable reason, to an iron stake in the dirt behind the Reps Theatre near Salisbury Service Station, where my father worked, my mother wasn't a flibbertijibbet or will-o'-the-wisp at all. As Sharon wandered too close and the bigger lion pounced on her, my mother leaped right onto that lion's back and tore him off by the ears. The one steely certainty about my mother was that she loved us absolutely.

She was born Joan Jackson, in South Africa, the second of two daughters—her well-to-do mother from celebrated 1820 settler stock; her Welsh father who had come to Johannesburg to work on the mines. Although they weren't Catholic, Joan and her older sister, Rosemarie, attended school at The Con- vent in Johannesburg, which was considered to be a refined education, and was where my mother studied her beloved ballet. Joan was perhaps ten when her father gambled their savings on a small mica mine close to Karoi, and he moved his family north to that hot flat blink of a Rhodesian town where the heat shimmered and wind scratched irritably against dry, lonely veldt. My mother's mouth twisted a little and she drew deeply on her cigarette when she remembered their "little gray home in the west." After holidays there, the train trip back to school in Johannesburg would take them three long days, she said, but after The Convent abruptly closed with a polio epidemic, my mother and her sister were hurriedly enrolled at Guinea Fowl, an all-boys rural boarding school where there were no other girls to giggle with and certainly no ballet. It was the only school in Rhodesia that had room for them on such short notice.

She never explicitly said as much, but my mother must have particularly hated Guinea Fowl after Rosemarie left and she was probably relieved, at seventeen, to graduate and finally join her sister in Salisbury. They both lived in a women's hostel— SACS House—my mother working as a clerk in town, typing and filing for the city council. Like all young white women in Salisbury in the 1950s, she probably played tennis in the late afternoon, then went to the movies or the odd party in the evening. Over the weekends there would have been cricket or rugby at the various sports clubs, with sundowners served by crisply dressed waiters afterward. The city then was neat and British, with stately colonial arches and wide cool verandas laid out sensibly. The buildings downtown were planned on a small grid with seven or eight main streets running from east to west and four or five from north to south. The avenues, all wide enough to turn an ox wagon, were mostly lined with trees, often jacarandas, which bloomed a bold mauve-blue in late September; my mother always remarked on their beauty with proprietary pride, as if she'd designed them herself.

Ian Black, a shy farm boy with a slight stammer, was among the group of friends my mother made at parties and club socials. One day a number of them signed up for ballroom dancing classes as a laugh. It didn't take long for the instructor to discover my mother's dancing talent. Ian, she noted, was athletic and agile too, so she paired them together. "Closer, closer!" she hollered above the strains of "The Last Waltz," finally slipping a vinyl record in between Joan and Ian's abdomens, forcing them to hold it there to create a perfect form. Joan smelled the light sweat on Ian's face. Ian shivered at the warm air from Joan's lips pulsing past his neck as they both panted "One-two-three, one-two-three." They could feel the shape of each other's body, soft around the firm disk.

By the time I was old enough to be curious, I knew better than to ask my father whether he had fallen in love with my mother after those ballroom dancing classes or whether he was smitten before. His old friend, Owen, confided that my mother was bewitchingly beautiful. My father's sister, Barbara, admitted that Joan changed the energy when she walked into a room. My uncle Alastair confessed unequivocally that from the first moment his brother Ian had laid eyes on Joan Jackson, he was instantly transfixed.

My father was always close to his family: two brothers and a sister. When I was young they got together regularly for tennis and afterward sipped cold Lion lager on the wide veranda, often chuckling fondly at childhood memories of playing on dirt courts, leaping from moving trains, or roaming the bush with their own *picanins*—black children my grandmother assigned to entertain them or to perform particular errands. My grand-

mother Katharine was a genteel Yorkshire woman caught uncertainly in England at the end of World War I. Her two elder
sisters were part of the old world, married off properly in the
Victorian manner; her two younger were part of the new and on
their way to Oxford. Katharine was neither here nor there; neither modern nor traditional, and so, perhaps searching for herself, she left England to teach art to young ladies in the then new
African colony called Rhodesia. After a number of years in Salisbury, she finally met a rough and humorless Scottish farmer
and was grateful, I think, to marry him, probably concerned by
then that her enormous weight would forever deter a suitor.

Katharine and Donald farmed a troublesome, barren tract
of land in the Gadzema district of Rhodesia. They had four
children: Barbara, another Donald, Ian (my father), and Alastair, all of whom Katharine tended to carefully and home-
schooled until they were quite old. Although the family
clearly struggled, Katharine's children always smiled when
they remembered their youth and were devastated when their
mother died suddenly before they were in their twenties. Her
tremendous bulk having taxed a system already weakened by
a debilitating bout of blackwater fever, a blood clot to her heart
killed her instantly.

Just seventeen and recently out of school, my father, who
particularly adored his mother, was lost after her death. He
took a job farming with Boss Lilford, the best tobacco grower
in the country, but hurriedly resigned after witnessing Lilford
brutally kick a pregnant black woman in the stomach. My
father wasn't shocked by racism—all Rhodesian settlers

believed themselves superior to blacks—but mostly their atti-
tude was paternalistic: a thin, sometimes irritable white tolerance for a clearly more primitive black race. Lilford's gratuitous
violence deeply offended my father, who quickly moved to
Salisbury, perhaps somewhat drawn by the knowledge that
natives, the polite term for black people then, lived there behind high walls in their own areas called townships and he
wouldn't have to put up with any more such nonsense.

My grandfather Donald, who had been notorious in
Gadzema for criticizing anyone who used more than one
square of toilet paper at a time and for working his laborers
seven days a week, became twice as crotchety after his wife's
death. He watched irritably as my father left Lilford and began to dither about his career: selling tobacco? back to farming? Repairing cars, Donald decided, anxious to end his son's
effortless town life. There was a good, rigorous course in mechanics at the Franklin Institute in Boston, which had the distinct added benefit of being far away from Ian's new girlfriend,
Joan, who was clearly leading him astray with her vivacious
eyes and suspiciously easy smile.

It took my father almost a month to make his way to the
coast of Africa and then sail to New York. After catching a train
north to Boston, he took a small room in a house on Newbury
Street for which he paid his landlady, Mrs. Davis, eight dollars
a week out of the money he made pumping gas. It was 1954.
He was a Rhodesian farm boy used to his own *picanin*, now
pumping gas through blistery cold nights for surly black truck
drivers. He used to mime for us how they wound their windows

down a crack to keep out the freezing wind, and then he narrowed his eyes and hissed their aggressive throaty growl, "Fill 'er up," chasing us as we laughed in delight and wonder, since in Rhodesia we'd only ever known black men to look down and clasp their hands when addressing my father, calling him *baas*.

By that first October in Boston, Mrs. Davis took pity on him and sewed buttons on his thin jacket. By November, he had booked his ticket home for two years hence, which he took out and stroked often, reassuring himself that his passage was certain. In February, he sent a letter proposing to Joan. In April, she accepted. For eternal miserable months after that, when he wasn't in class or pumping gas, he tossed with insomnia or sat at the small desk of his cold room, fantasizing about his future, recording in endless journals his desperate and all-consuming love: *Few attain the heights and utter bliss of true love; mere books, prose, poetry, and song have been written about so-called love—how abused and cheap it is all made to be!* Mrs. Davis would knock on his door, reminding him to come to dinner. Her daughter, Ailine, flirted shyly with him at first and then increasingly boldly. For my father's last few months in the United States, Ailine Davis angrily refused to speak to him at all.

When Ian finally returned to Rhodesia in the middle of 1956, he wasted no more time. He got a job repairing cars at Salisbury Service Station, bought a small square house with a tennis court and swimming pool in a tidy suburb called Mount Pleasant, planted a tall prickly hedge, a rose garden, and a bank of flowering cherries there, and married Joan in October; a few years after that, first I, then Sharon, and finally Lauren, was born.

• • •

WHEN I WAS VERY YOUNG, MY MOTHER WOULD INVITE PEOPLE
over to our small house in Mount Pleasant for a casual *braai*, a
barbecue, and then open the front door wearing a midnight-
blue velvet dress with her dark hair scooped up into a rhine-
stone tiara. The dress had hung in the bathroom beforehand
amid billowing clouds of steam from the shower turned on full:
a nipped and sensuous skirt supported by a boned and strap-
less bodice, assertive ghostly breasts looming over me as I peed.

She really wanted to be a ballerina. She had an old vinyl
record of *Swan Lake*, with a picture of pink ballet slippers on
its worn soft cover, that she played regularly. "Come," she
panted, pulling at me when the opening bars of the "Dance of

My mother, Sharon, and me.

the Cygnets" rattled our glass doors. I'd glance down quickly to avoid her funny thumb (they'd had to chop a bit off it when she got a rose thorn stuck under her nail) and join her in those funny cygnet steps, and fall about laughing or beg her to "twist again," and we would pretend to dry ourselves with towels. But after a short while she would always put *Swan Lake* back on, loud and tinny, and eventually I'd wander off, bored.

She wasn't like the other mothers I knew. She poked a python out of our hedge with a broom. She yelled "Jump!" when the swing was at its highest, bit into onions like apples, and tried to convince me that it was *always* better to have flowers than food. Before Chirstmas we peeked, whispering, mischievous, conspiratorial, at my new dollhouse through the keyhole of the garage. Once we ate sweets together until I threw up. She didn't care whether Sharon wore clothes and was happy to cut up her own satin wedding dress to make gowns for my dolls—she sewing and chatting, me chewing the wax flowers of her bridal headpiece flat and spitting them out in a neat gray pile on her bed.

One day in the car, I whimsically mentioned I wanted to ride the grimy African bus ahead of us, and she promptly waved it down, bossily ignoring the snarled traffic and the astonished face of the black driver, pushing me, a five-year-old white child, through the soft black flesh and colorful bundles of alarmed passengers, hollering at my back to look out for her through the rear window. The bus stank of sweat and diesel. Yet hotter air pumped through its dirty windows as the bus pulled into traffic and I made a circle in the grimy glass and saw my mother there, waving to me encouragingly from our pale blue Cortina.

She followed me in her car through the clean white suburbs of Avondale and Milton Park, where the houses had
lawns and swimming pools and tennis courts and the bus
jolted and roared, stopping and starting, flesh and bundles
shifting and resettling, stirring sweat, as people heaved on and
off at neat and efficient shopping centers. Downtown, we
turned onto First Street, where there were banks and teashops,
offices and department stores, and white people strolled the
recently swept pavements. First Street ended in the Cow's
Guts, the dirtier Indian part of town. Here, storekeepers set
up stalls outside their small shops or strung bright merchan-
dise from awnings and noisily hawked their wares to African
women, who hunted through their own expansive cleavages
for carefully hidden cash. Beyond the Cow's Guts, the bus
depot was on the lip of the Industrial Sites—a frantic fume-
thick place, where a baffling number of blacks milled and
yelled, deciphering schedules or selling single cigarettes and
oranges. The bus I was on disgorged me there, and I flowed out
onto the filthy sidewalk, where I was assaulted by dust and the
odor of burning rubber and rotting fruit. Then my mother
appeared, smilingly pushing her way through jostling crowds,
laughing at my bewilderment, scooping me up against the
starched cotton of her dress and the wires in her undergar-
ments, the soft skin of her strong arms folded across my back,
her body smelling salty and sweet, like home.

MY FATHER WAS PROUD OF RHODESIA'S UNILATERAL DECLARA-
tion of Independence from Great Britain in 1965. He drank to

UDI at our *braais* and tennis parties where, after a few beers, he would often say, "Wendy, tell us about UDI," and on cue I would sing out, "Rhodesia has sanctions, and I can't have Marmite on my toast!" Then he would chortle with delight, grabbing and tousling my hair while the other grown-ups laughed.

I had no idea what sanctions or UDI really meant. In 1966, a year after the declaration, I was equally oblivious to the incident in which Rhodesian Security Forces killed seven black guerrillas, marking the beginning of the Rhodesian War. That same year my mother brought Lauren home in her yellow carry-cot from the Lady Chancellor maternity hospital in Salisbury, where it was rumored they used placentas to fertilize the extravagant roses on their grounds. About then the threads that held our lives together slowly began to fray.

Some months after Lauren's birth, my mother began to retreat into puzzling, cigarette-waving moods. I started to discover empty bottles of gin or cane spirit hidden among her underwear. Often, she simply locked herself in her bedroom and cried. I would post myself outside her door, anxiously listening for movement or for her potential small requests, while Sharon sat close to me, chubby knees drawn into her naked brown body, sucking hard on her thumb.

Sometimes, when no sound came from my mother's bedroom at all, Sharon and I wandered out to the *kaya*, a tiny brick or concrete building built off at a discreet distance from the main house, where Margaret, Josiah, and Isaac lived. My parents told us it was dirty there, and we weren't supposed to go in. Sometimes my father had to check whether the servants had visitors living there illegally, and we heard him yelling

angrily, demanding *situpas*, special African identification papers, if they did. Occasionally, he even called the police.

After my father would go to work, though, Margaret usually
strapped Lauren onto her back with towels like an African
baby, so she could clean the house and polish the floor, and
then matter-of-factly took her back to the *kaya* for tea.
Sharon and I followed them there, squatting around the fire,
looking from face to face as people we didn't know laughed
and shouted in Shona to each other; we stuck our uninvited
hands into the three-legged black cast-iron *sadza* pot to grab
chunks of warm, gritty cornmeal porridge that tasted of smoke.

When we wanted attention we'd ask, "But *why* do you have
your bed up on all those bricks, Margaret?" knowing that
would make everybody stop and whistle and click their
tongues and say *eee weh* and *my wei*, while we'd just smile innocently. We knew the bricks were there because Margaret
and everyone else were afraid of *tokoloshies*.

We used the *tokoloshies* as an excuse to rummage through
Margaret's things—scratching through cardboard drawers
and tattered envelopes, imagining we might find fairies and
elves. One time I snapped open her plastic handbag and saw
my grandmother's crystal pendant glinting against the dark
bottom. I snapped the bag quickly shut again and walked
slowly back to the house with my heart beating hard before
softly opening my mother's bedroom door. "Mummy," I said
quietly. Her eyes flickered open and I said urgently, "I think
Margaret stole Granny's necklace." I felt particularly responsible since Granny had lent her pendant to *me* after weeks of
tugging and whining. "Please just go," my mother said thickly,

closing her waxy eyes again, leaving me standing there with a sense of something heavy in my arms.

Some days, my mother came out of her room and swept through the house, tidying and reorganizing, once stuffing me, dirty and barefoot, into the basket on the shocked drugstore deliveryman's scooter and sending me, with an impatient note, to my father at work.

Occasionally, she was more like her old self. When I got a concussion after falling off my bike, she waited until the nurse walked away before gently moving the greasy EEG electrodes aside to speak softly in my ear. "Think like crazy for a few seconds, then clear your head, then think like crazy, then clear your head, like a light switch—*on-off-on-off-on-off*. That'll confuse them," she advised.

Once, at Highlands Junior School sports day, she came to watch as I stumbled over hurdles, dropped beanbags, and only struggled my feet into the sack long after most of my teammates had hopped across the finish line. The kids from the Grenville and Nelson teams laughed at me and cheered. The Drake kids glared with sullen white faces under their floppy red hats. Humiliated and dejected, I dragged myself to my mother, who wiped my face and smiled at me with shiny love reflected in the bottom of her unusually clear eyes. "I have a special prize for you," she said, feeling at the foot of Lauren's carry-cot; then she kissed me gently as she wrapped my hand around a delicate glass fawn.

On my seventh birthday, she bought me a thrilling crinoline doll birthday cake with a scalloped pink-frosting skirt,

Sharon, Lauren, and me in 1966.

blond plastic hair, and a red painted smile on its lips. I was to take it to school, where she drove me that morning in my father's brand-new Ford Mustang that he had imported especially from America. There was no warning gasp before we sailed off the road, floating, it seemed, until glass shattered and metal crushed, the car hissing viciously against a stone gatepost, Mum's unconscious body flopped deafeningly on the horn. After a few moments of that eerie steam and wail, the cool African morning burst with voices shouting and brakes squealing, the damaged door of the car yanked open, and people yelled urgently at one another. They pulled her out and carried her away like a thirties movie star, arms, head, dark hair, and high-heeled sandals all dangling down. I waited, uncertain, in the backseat while voices receded until finally my father came and gently pried my birthday cake out of my hands (taking care not to damage the frosting) and, murmuring and reassuring, drove me the rest of the way to school.

After my birthday that year, we took my mother down to a special hospital in South Africa. My father took care to unscrew the inside handles from all the car's doors before propping my mother, breathing but lifeless, in the front seat. Sharon and I followed in a car behind them, and although I don't recall if Lauren was there or who drove us, the anxieties of watching the back of my parents' car disappear and reappear on the curling road ahead is still vivid and strong. In Johannesburg, we stayed with too-cheerful strangers who spoke to us loudly as if we didn't quite understand English and fed us at their kitchen table with bread and butter and salty tomato soup. My father took me to visit with my mother's old ballet teacher, Maree. She was my godmother, and I'd been named Wendy Maree in homage, although I didn't remember her from before and never saw her again after that day. Her studio was rosin-scented with a honey-colored floor and the sun sparkled in mirrors, which also reflected rainbows of pastel tutus dangling upside down from racks on wheels, like vast tulle bats. I rubbed the soft pink ribbon from a ballet slipper with my thumb and watched Maree and my father whisper together, able only to hear the words *shock treatment*. I was glad my mother was being cared for, not knowing then— buzzing, jolting, gnashing, peeing, and then limp and drooling—that the treatment would destroy part of her brain.

My mother was away for what felt like a long time, but she didn't come home better. I still waited outside her bedroom for the sound of breathing or tears, and she still frightened me with her slurring ash-flicking moods. I worried about Lauren, still a baby, now in the *kaya* all the time. My father seemed to spend longer and longer hours at Salisbury Service Station, and when he did come home my parents fought, disappearing for long hours behind loveless slammed doors.

One night when I was almost eight, Sharon and I were sitting on the floor in front of *Batman* on TV, eating our everyday supper, a large plate of fat French fries and tomato sauce that Josiah had prepared before he left, when the doorbell rang. I ran to answer it and found a stranger there holding Lauren, who was blinking her round brown eyes in the soft outside light. Lauren's pale hair grew surprised-straight on her head, her sweet pudgy feet, mouth, and the seat of her yellow pajamas all grubby with red African dust, and she was clutching at the blouse of this unknown woman who had brought her home.

"Hello," the woman finally said, when she realized no one else was coming. "I found this baby wandering down the side of the road." She looked past me hopefully again. "Do you know where she belongs?"

I stared at the woman's concerned face and then at Lauren, who squirmed restlessly on her hip, and felt a twinge of alarm. My father was still at work. My mother had been in her bedroom all day. "She belongs here," I said finally, reaching out to take my little sister, holding her soft body tightly in my arms, aware of our hearts beating loudly and close.

4

Our mother's words had an anarchic, ethereal quality, always refusing to stick to anything, so I didn't believe her when she warned there was going to be a divorce. I should have known when Sharon, Lauren, and I moved with her into the Bronte Boarding Hotel, where we all shared one big double bed and would spoon soup out of clumsy china plates in the echoing dining room. But so much about our mother was erratic and unpredictable. The Bronte, with its high white walls, wide arches, and long cool verandas, simply seemed like another event on an unfathomable continuum that our dad did nothing to explain when we saw him on occasional weekends.

The Bronte felt like a place where people were supposed to wait—like a hospital, or a train station at midnight—but no one wanted to wait there for long. I tried to cheer my mother up by recruiting Sharon and Lauren to wrap up soap and toothpaste for her birthday, but when she cried so hard on opening our gifts, we were terrified at the sight of her shoulders shaking in such violent, shuddering jags.

Our meals grew stranger: chips or peanuts for breakfast, a packet of dry soup for lunch. When I went to school I got into trouble for arriving to class late, wearing a pink anorak and with my hair disheveled. Everyone else had pigtails, and the Highlands Junior School colors were red and gray.

Our mother did have happy days, when the four of us went to bed early and took turns adding parts to long hilarious stories. Even Lauren, who was just two then (although no one had remembered her birthday), caught some of the jokes and contributed her own funny bits. But when my mother was sad, the Bronte was even lonelier. Holding Lauren's little hand, Sharon and I would wander the grounds, which were lush with sweet frangipani and waving palms. Starlings argued in the hedges, wagtails wagged in the shrubs, and happy bulbuls splashed in the birdbath. But there weren't any other children there, and the adults, who idled in the dining room or on the benches in the shade, had an unreassuring transience behind their smiles.

Even though I sensed we were waiting for something, I was still surprised when it happened. One day, my father picked me up from Highlands and as we drove alone in his car he stared straight ahead and unequivocally announced that he and my mother were divorced. Still eight, I sat there and said nothing at all. Clearing his throat as we approached the construction site of our new house, he told me, his words still solid and certain, that he had permanent custody of us. I tried to cry, squeezing my eyes tightly together to force a little juice out of them, if only because my mother had said that I should. "Cry loudly," she had instructed. "Make sure you stamp and kick when he tells you," she had gone on to add, pursing her lips and looking upward, wondering how else to make the point.

But secretly I was happy that my father was now in charge and we only had to see our mother every second weekend.

HE WANTED A BRITISH GOVERNESS FOR US. GOV-ERN-ESS. I ROLLED the word on my tongue, and it sounded orderly and reassuring. I had never heard of anyone in Rhodesia having a governess, but I had read about those delightfully predictable women in books. It seemed only appropriate, now that we were about to move into a mansion to start a new and tidy life. Our dad had made a lot of money through savvy business dealings during the time we had lived in Mount Pleasant. At first, he borrowed money to establish a secondhand car lot opposite Salisbury Service Station. As years went by, he opened a string of used-car lots downtown. Then he opened Salisbury Financial Holdings in order to process car install-ment purchases independently, and then, based on the prom-ise of all those future repayments, he borrowed vast sums of money from the bank to put into brilliant schemes right away. All our friends and relatives, and even little old ladies who didn't know him, thought he was a genius and poured their nest eggs into his ideas. He bought a ranch down south, in Matabeleland. He bought a small media group in Salisbury. He invested heavily in a big earthmoving company and signed a lucrative contract to build roads out in Mount Darwin, one of Rhodesia's more remote rural areas, signing off on that huge loan with his personal guarantee, daringly balancing his business empire so that one investment supported the other, like a row of dominoes. The last domino would ring a bell, and the bell was Bien Donné, our big hexagonal house on the hill.

Sharon and I in the garden at Bien Donné.

He called the *big house* (as our mother spitefully dubbed it) or *home* (as he angrily insisted) Bien Donné, because he said that meant "well given" in French, and he believed the house was. The years in Boston, the long period of establishing himself in business, and the trauma of my mother were finally over. Now there was something to show for it: piped music throughout, a formal living room (where children were not allowed), a formal dining room (not there either), a bar (that was always locked so the servants couldn't steal the alcohol and the children couldn't steal the cashews from Mozambique or the chocolates from South Africa), and a billiard room decorated with the skins and heads and feet and skulls of animals my dad had shot (where the children weren't allowed unless expressly invited, and even then not anywhere near the billiard table).

We also had an indoor fountain with flowing water and cascading plants, a grand piano, a tennis court, a squash court, a swimming pool, a sauna, and acres of beautifully landscaped gardens planted with sweet gardenias, deeply purple irises, bright bougainvilleas, heavy honeysuckle, alert strelitzias, and juicy pomegranate trees. Bien Donné was the site of lots of parties with laughing, beautiful women and fairy lights in the tall leafy msasas. The rose garden that my dad pruned every Rhodes and Founders, a public holiday in July to celebrate Cecil John Rhodes's "discovery" of Rhodesia, was heavy with blooms. We had a rambling system of interconnecting ponds full of tadpoles to catch in jam jars, noisy bullfrogs to lull us to sleep at night, and a waterfall made of amethyst crystals, the purpleness of which you seldom saw because it was always slimy with algae. Of course we had plenty of servants to perpetually scrub the waterfall, to sweep the blond river of pale sand endlessly up the steeply inclined driveway (my dad didn't like the blackness of asphalt), and to peel the grapes (although children had to peel their own).

By the time I settled in to Bien Donné, where the clean light rang like glass and loping black gardeners pushed wheelbarrows in the sun, I had learned from my parents, as they had learned from theirs, not to think too closely about race. When I was about nine my English cousin came to visit, and his mother took us to the nearby Newlands Shopping Center. The place was uncharacteristically busy with coughing buses and bicycles, arguing vendors, and late commuters hurrying back to wherever they needed to be after some unusual event in our white suburb. My cousin said excitedly, "Mummy, Mummy, look at all the people!" Confused, I stared out over the milling black heads and asked, "Where?"

I'M NOT CERTAIN THAT THE KIND OF BRITISH GOVERNESS MY father had in mind existed by the late sixties, even in England. He would eventually abandon his illusions and turn to Chum and Anne, his best friend Owen's parents, who still farmed in Gadzema close to where my father had grown up but who were now delighted to retreat from what had been a challenging rural life. Chum shuffled around Bien Donné, clutching a cigar with a curling end of ash and a brandy and soda that he put down (and forgot) whenever he went to the toilet. Or he roamed our enormous garden with a .22, sending giant African bullfrogs flying out of the algae and tiny butcher-birds falling out of the trees. (Those frogs were bloody noisy and those birds—well, they might look innocent, but they would have every other bird in our garden pinned to thorns if he let them have their way, Chum explained.) Sometimes Chum was summoned by Granny Anne to take us to school or to an activity, a task he would embark on purposefully, sitting forward in his seat, nose close to the windscreen of his tan Ford Anglia, a common little car in Rhodesia then that was designed with shock absorbers inadequate for harsh African roads.

Granny Anne was a cheerful Afrikaans woman with a thin graying ponytail and flat empty breasts that fell heavily on her fleshy waist. She sometimes sucked her false teeth away from her old gums, which made us squeal in horror. Her laugh was a deep tummy-jiggling one. I know my father was probably dubious of all the sweet Afrikaans food Anne introduced into the house, like creamy *melktert* and *koeksisters* that would pop with rivers of cane sugar syrup in your mouth and make you cough with their intensity, and that he worried, us being of British origin, that we might pick up her thick Afrikaans accent (so déclassé!), but he was grateful overall for the strong sense of warmth and order she gave to our new mansion.

We moved far away from the life of endless french fries and no bedtimes we'd experienced with our mother. In its place, Lauren went neatly washed to nursery school. Sharon and I went to Highlands every day with sandwiches and braids. Granny Anne arranged ballet, tennis, piano, and elocution lessons. My father was very interested in maintaining our lips pursed in a proper British *o*, rather than let them relax into a lazy line that squeezed vowels flat and rolled out *r*'s into Granny Anne–influenced sentences like *Hey, ja, man it's lekker-r-r hey*, which meant something was good; or *Ye-e-s-okay-no-fine*, which meant a halfhearted *yes*. Our elocution teacher gave us candy if we e-nun-ci-a-ted our words, stale pink marshmallow fish, long flat pieces of licorice, sherbet in packets, or black gobstoppers that turned different colors as you sucked them smaller. My father hit me only once and it was for not speaking prop-er-ly. He had me by the arm but I was able to run my legs forward and arch my back so he mostly swatted at fresh air, but it still stopped me from saying *ja, man* within his hearing again.

Sometimes our father took us away for weekends, mostly to Kariba, the enormous inland sea the government created by damming the powerful Zambezi River, one of the country's proudest accomplishments. More than once, as children, we filed reverently into Highlands Junior School hall and sat wide-eyed and cross-legged on the cold linoleum floor to watch the whirring grainy black-and-white film of *Operation Noah*, which showed brave game wardens efficiently steering elephants and buffalos through the newly dammed and rapidly rising waters to safer shores, sedating antelopes and zebras and lifting them, with their leaden, feebly protesting heads, onto wobbly boats.

It was a five-hour drive from Salisbury to Lake Kariba. When we turned off at Makuti there was a plummeting road that switched and turned, leaving behind the cooler highveld and dropping into the steamy Zambezi valley. Sharon,

Lauren, and I were usually bickering and pushing in the backseat by then, each desperate to be the first to see the lake, tortured because we were so close, and yet my dad had to drive very slowly in case he surprised a herd of elephant around one of those sharp blind bends.

Kariba is malaria ridden. And it's so hot that when they were building the dam wall they had to keep their tools in buckets of water so they could be handled. But in spite of the heat and mosquitoes, and in spite of the fact that Sharon and I had once gone with my father on a holiday in Spain (Lauren had been too little and was left behind), we still agreed that we loved Kariba the most. We sat up front on *Show Girl*, my father's motorboat, our skinny burnt shoulders hunched in anticipation, and we went fast, bouncing hard on our bony bottoms over the wake. In the late afternoons, we ate Willards chips and swam in the hot green pool at the Lake View Hotel, still wearing floppy farmer's hats even in the water, sliding wantonly down the rusty pool slide, glancing at our father, out of earshot on the veranda, and then abandoning our elocution, happily pronouncing *swim* as *swum*, forbidden Rhodesian expressions like *mushi hey?* and *lekker-r man!* splashing from our mouths.

WE SAW MY MOTHER EVERY OTHER WEEKEND, AS THE COURTS had decided, though she phoned Bien Donné often. Granny Anne spent long hours talking to her, listening to her long sad stories, cooing at her tears, and arranging little rendezvous where we all could meet outside of the cold judge-imposed rules. Sometimes, Anne and Chum took my mother with us when we went up to Glengyll, their little farm in Gadzema, for the weekend. Being with my mother was still almost fun— if there were other, real, adults close by. Anne and Chum's bare-bones farmhouse smelled of butter biscuits and kerosene, and we'd sleep on low beds in a room with dusty pictures of angels hovering over small children about to get themselves into trouble. Geckos and spiders rustled in the molding thatch or scuttled behind the pictures or into the shadows that the hissing gaslight threw on the walls, while our mother folded our clothes, read us stories, or brushed our hair.

Back at Bien Donné, it was a relief to have Granny Anne pay particular attention to Lauren, smiling at her tenderly, calling her Lollipop, and laughing satisfying belly laughs at her sweet baby sayings. She lured Lauren up the kitchen stairs when it got late with soft twangy words, coaxing her with Bovril toast, or some grated biltong, and then lay next to her as Lauren fell asleep curled up in Granny Anne's own warm bed. I noticed how, hours later, when Granny Anne finally went to bed herself, she didn't move Lauren. She simply slipped under the blankets and wrapped herself around Lauren's little body protectively, holding her tightly all night.

One night, I shook Granny Anne awake. "My pajama pants are too tight," I whined pitifully, hoping she would either move over and let me climb in alongside Lauren or turn on a low, intimate light and whisper and fuss close-headed with me in my closet. But she only blinked crossly. "Well, change them, then," she mumbled, spitting through empty gums, and so with a pang of humiliation, I crept back to my lonely room.

I felt empty, as though I was missing something important, and started to cling rather pathetically to my father's girl-friends. There was Shirley, who took us away for weekends and gave us hot chocolate; Marlene, who taught us how to do flying ballet leaps on the lawn; Jackie, who brought us a little Pomeranian puppy that whimpered all night in my room; Carol, who had a deep suntan and spoke French; and Harriet, who had enormous breasts and caused my father's friends to fight with their wives.

After years of being shy, my father was now emboldened by his new wealthy-bachelor status, even prodding me to ask my teachers for dates on his behalf.

"Just tell her I think she's pretty," he would bend down and say into my ear, looking at Miss Johnson in her short miniskirt and long black hair, his big hand in the small of my back, nudging me in her direction.

"No!" I batted him off, eyes half frowning, mouth half smiling, happy to be included in a grown-up game.

Gail was by far the youngest and most beautiful of the women our father brought home. She floated into Bien Donné clutching his strong arm, buoyed on a cloud of teasing light-heartedness, pulling his tall body closer and closer, then push-ing him back and back, tossing her beautiful blond hair onto his broad shoulders, whispering from a place deep in her throat. I watched her carefully as she held up our new paint-ings against the wall—"A little to the right; maybe farther down; I think more this way," my father instructed her, frown-ing absorbedly.

"Is your father always like this?" She laughed, noticing me

staring at her, drawing me into an irresistible aura of *us grown-up women,* sighingly tolerant at the inadequacies of men.

On the weekends we didn't go to our mother, I began to wait for Gail. I prepared songs to sing to her. I sat in my room making little mementos for her flat in the Avenues. She taught me how to smile like a movie star. "Too much gum," she said, shaking her head as I grinned hopefully at her. I practiced for hours in the bathroom mirror, trying to push my smile down on my face: not letting my top lip go up too far, pulling my bottom lip lower to show half my bottom teeth, squaring off the corners of my mouth.

Sometimes, on Sundays, she took me to mass with her, leaving Sharon and Lauren at home. My father was a perfunctory Presbyterian and my mother only later mentioned God, so I had never been to church. Gail would lend me a black mantilla she kept wrapped in tissue and we lit candles, kneeling devoutly, softly rattling pearly rosary beads, intimate in the clouds of incense.

My father worried a bit that I didn't play with children my own age. Once, he came up to my room, as he always did at night, and after we chatted awhile he paused, then said gently, "Why don't you invite some little girls over to play sometime?"

"I like being by myself," I replied, suddenly alert to a possible shortcoming I didn't know I had. He thoughtfully stroked the blue cloth cover of a book he held in his lap.

"Maybe you should read this," he suggested abruptly, handing me a copy of *How to Win Friends and Influence People* before quickly kissing me good night.

Sensing his embarrassment, I felt I'd let him down. Still, I never told him that I did have a friend. I was at a new private senior school by then, where Cynthia and I scrambled to sit together in class and at lunch or dawdled in the changing room, giggling in our ridiculous swim caps. After tea, we always sat cross-legged under minty-blue gum trees with half a dozen other girls and played a clapping game: slapping out a beat on our own knees, singing "Who put the cookie in the cookie jar?" and then each naming different girls in the circle. When I got home at night I used to imitate Dorothy, a black girl (private schools were allowed to enroll 6 percent nonwhite) by pushing out my lips and crossing my eyes, clapping my hands on my knees and missing, slurring a half-witted African accent. It made my dad and Gail laugh lovingly and allowed me to stay close to them for a little longer before they told me to go and play. But I would have been embarrassed if Cynthia knew I ridiculed Dorothy like that. And having anyone at Bien Donné know my best friend was an Indian would certainly have been disappointing—a failure of sorts, like not being good at athletics—so I made excuses when she invited me to the movies or to the new ice rink, not wanting to be seen in public with her, preferring not even to think about Cynthia outside of school.

Gratefully, my father never mentioned my lack of friends again, and on the weekends at Bien Donné I continued to amuse myself in my bedroom or to hover around Gail. Often, when we had parties, she came over early to help with the details and then got ready at the softly lit dressing table in my dad's room. I would kneel down next to her and watch carefully as she lined her eyes and dusted her cheekbones, leaning forward, pouting open-mouthed to apply a ravishing pinkness to her lips. After dropping her robe, she stepped delicately into tiny panties, bent slightly at the waist to shake her breasts into a satiny bra, and pulled on a narrow cat suit made of revealing white lace. I stared at how beautiful she was, awed at her boldness and daring. When she held her heavy hair aside for me to fasten the clasp at the top, I could smell the talcum powder brushed lightly along her neck. I worshiped her.

OUR FATHER MARRIED GAIL ON AUGUST 14, 1971, IN THE OLD Presbyterian Church on Enterprise Road (the Catholic church refused to marry a divorced man) and the celebration afterward was at Bien Donné. Caterers set up white-covered tables on the lawn overlooking the valley. The florist made an enormous Styrofoam board to float in our hexagon-shaped pool, secured with thin fishing wire that spelled out IAN AND GAIL in carnations. Smaller boards in the shape of hearts floated in its orbit. Gail's three sisters were bridesmaids in purple; Sharon, Lauren, Gail's niece Charlaine, and I were flower girls in lilac.

Sharon, Lauren, and I were permitted into the billiard room only because it was a good vantage point from which to wave at my father's white Mercedes as they left the next day on their honeymoon. Just before pulling away, Gail scrambled out of the car and invited us to come along. "We can't leave them behind," she said, shrugging helplessly at my father as we galloped off to pack.

Lauren, my dad, me, Gail, and Sharon.

So the whole brand-new family drove up to the Montclair Hotel in Inyanga, in the eastern highlands of the country, my dad booming out "Grandmother's Chair" and "Molly Malone," his lips pursed, his hands as expressive as an Italian tenor. We could see by the way he looked at Gail that he loved her deeply, and he announced to all of us that he was now going to spend more time with his family. "Dave can handle the office," he said happily, and Gail held her hand tenderly on his thigh, laughing as he roared out his songs, turning around to roll her eyes conspiratorially with us as we giggled with her from the backseat.

And as we drove higher into the purple mist and rocks, passing apple trees and scrubby everlasting flowers, I eagerly agreed to keep Lauren busy, once we got to the Montclair, with Ping-Pong in the games room or long walks to see the slave-hut ruins. I knew Gail was still annoyed that Lauren had pulled out her carefully pinned and sprayed coif just before the wedding, running around like the wild girl from Borneo, almost ruining the photographs, making everyone late.

Lauren wouldn't prove to be more cooperative. That first night, after I helped her brush her teeth and find her nightgown, she tore off the sweetly engraved silver St. Christopher medal that Gail had given her for a bridesmaid present and dropped it in the dustbin.

"Lol! You'll get into trouble," I warned, panicked at the possibility of her upsetting the equilibrium in our new picture-perfect family.

"Don't care," Lauren said, flouncing into her high hotel bed, not even glancing at the half-buried pendant among dirty tissues and hairballs, where Gail discovered it in the morning, just catching the light, glinting up at her defiantly.

BIEN DONNÉ WAS NOT BIG ENOUGH FOR TWO WOMEN TO RUN it. Gail was furious when Granny Anne contradicted her instructions to the servants, and Granny Anne was maddened when Gail introduced her as "the housekeeper," so Chum and Anne left just six months after the wedding. By that time Lauren was already five years old, but as I watched her crying on the wide sandy driveway of our big house, she suddenly seemed too small and alarmingly alone. Something anxious clutched in my chest, so I quickly looked away from her to wave at Granny Anne, who was sniffing too, wiping her eyes and sucking up her teeth so they didn't fall down as she breathed through her sad open mouth. Grampa Chum sat forward in his seat, nose close to the windscreen of his little car, as he always did.

My father kept his word and began to come home for long leisurely lunches. He returned to Bien Donné again by five o'clock every afternoon, when Sharon, Lauren, and I would pull at him to play tag in the pool or beg him to push us high on the swing.

Gail tried hard to be a good stepmother: a girly confidante for Sharon and me; quick to defend Lauren in playground squabbles or against a teacher's oversight. But for whatever human reason, Gail and Lauren were never able to touch any true chord in the other's heart, and they circled each other warily, always a little closer to being enemies than they ever were to being friends.

One day, after Gail and my father had been married close to a year, the nanny came to the veranda door with three streaks of blood beading and glistening on her cheek. "Lauren she is scratching," the woman reported without emotion. Lauren stood behind her, her arms folded, glaring out from under thick dark brows. Dad quickly picked her up by one arm and smacked her hard on the bottom. I watched, almost crying myself, but Lauren didn't even whimper, just as she didn't flinch at the hiding she got when she threw our Pomeranian puppy on the floor in a rash of temper. Both times she tilted her chin and walked slowly past us and stubbornly up the stairs, all by herself.

Gail seemed increasingly grateful to leave most of the serious parenting to my father. She conferred with him about dentists and haircuts but really preferred to busy herself in other ways. Eager to prove herself capable as a young wife, she learned how to arrange flowers. She learned how to drive. She saved the monthly allowance my father gave her and bought a secondhand freezer. She took cooking lessons from a fat Hungarian woman who came to Bien Donné with ingredients brimming from her canvas bag, a wet patch on the back of her skirt marking a weak bladder.

Still, despite Gail's pains to convey maturity and sophistication, my father's family often teased her. At dinner parties with Auntie Barbara, my father's sister, and Mark, her husband, a Rhodesian government cabinet minister, even Dad couldn't suppress giggles as they dryly mocked Gail's South African accent: the way she said *yooman* instead of *human*, with the requisite puff of air along with the *h*. Sometimes Mark ahemmed, adjusted his monocle, and asked her loud questions like, "And what does *your* father do, Gail?" leaving her stammering selfconsciously, ashamed to say *used-car salesman* to a member of the cabinet. As the evening progressed and conversation got more boisterous, everyone toasted UDI and Gail shrank back a little, sipping a watery Coke. Not interested in politics, she smiled sweetly as my father turned to Mark for the inside story on the war, only half-listening to Mark explaining that there wasn't really a war at all. In 1971 the Rhodesian government was still firmly in control of any black troublemakers.

When Gail did try to participate, her nervousness tended to make things worse. Once, over coffee, Mark carefully recounted a long story about a black woman on his farm who was doing her laundry in the river when she was taken by a crocodile. The woman was at a particular part of the river when she put her soap down on a particular rock and leaned over at a particular angle before the great scaly animal lurched up and snatched her. Not really caring about the black woman, everyone was silent. Gail, however, wondered if she had missed something important. "But Mark," she broke in seriously. "What happened to the soap?"

IN 1972, JUST AFTER A FAILED PEACE INITIATIVE, THE FIRST Rhodesian farmers were killed at their lonely homesteads, initiating a barrage of terrifying rural terrorist attacks and ambushes on whites. The war, everyone agreed, had really begun. That same year, Gail and my father's daughter, Shiobhan, was born. The sweetest and most placid little baby, Shiobhan provoked doting smiles from Gail and Dad, who posed for tender pictures holding her. Lauren, now six, was no longer the youngest in the family and lost whatever small privilege or sympathy that status had once conferred.

Shiobhan brought on a dizzy reshuffling of affection. Sharon and I anxiously washed pacifiers, folded diapers, and offered pillows or glasses of cold water to Gail while she nursed, nervously trying to hold on to our own little pieces of love. And as Shiobhan grew, we entertained her, played with her, and took care of her while the nanny was at lunch when Gail asked us to. One afternoon while Gail was napping,

Shiobhan hit her forehead on the swing and almost instanta-
neously was covered in blood. Horrified, I rushed her into the
house. "But weren't you taking care of her?" Gail shouted,
flashing me a bewildering stare as she snatched her baby. I sat
on the edge of the toilet with my throat closing slowly, riv-
eted, terrified by something far bigger than Shiobhan's injury,
as Gail shook and sobbed and tenderly washed Shiobhan's
face over the bathtub, thankfully revealing just a tiny cut.

Lauren watched too, silent as a shadow, too small to fold
diapers properly or carry water without spilling. Gail and my
father had less time now to discuss Lauren's behavior or to
listen to her as she practiced reading. If she had a tantrum,
which she did much more rarely now, someone usually called
for Nelly, the nanny, to take her away. When she gagged on a
piece of hot pineapple in the Hungarian lady's fancy Chinese
Chicken, she refused to touch the rest of her dinner. Sam, the
cook, was instructed to serve it for her breakfast, and then
again for lunch. Lauren sat in front of that congealed plate,
passive eyes stormy, until everyone got impatient with teaching her a lesson and she slipped, unnoticed and forgotten,
from her chair.

By 1973 my father became increasingly less tolerant of
dinnertime dramas. Every evening, he anxiously turned on
the TV to listen to the newscaster for the Rhodesian Broadcasting Corporation tell solemn stories of terrorists training
in Zambia and bloody atrocities perpetrated on Rhodesian
farms. When Barbara and Mark came over for dinner, Mark
reminded everyone that the emergency legislation imposed

after UDI was rigorous and should contain any discontent, but by now he seemed less certain.

Portuguese colonists lost control of neighboring Mozambique in 1974, and the country's new black government, like Zambia's, permitted a number of terrorist training camps, effectively opening a second front. Shortly thereafter, my father was served with his first call-up papers, instructing him to perform six weeks of military duty monitoring guerrilla activity in one of the Tribal Trust Lands, the vast empty tracts of barren country that had been allocated, years before, to blacks.

My father was a fastidious man, used to the clean predictability of Bien Donné and Salisbury, so he hated those interminable days spent on hard bald ground, with cicadas shrieking, dust choking every throat, and dry broken cornstalks flickering in the harsh light. One stultifying afternoon he rested, slightly thinner and unshaven, against an old syringa tree and watched curiously as a light aircraft dropped out of the sky and bounced to a sudden standstill nearby. Wondering if he were dreaming, my father watched the plane door open and the director of Salisbury Financial Holdings emerge uncertainly into the intense heat, the edge of the man's dark suit and briefcase rippling, a black hallucination suspended against a white sun.

My father had two more weeks in the bush to absorb the implications of his director's urgent message that terrorist activity coupled with land mines dotting rural tracks in the Mount Darwin area were leaving his huge earthmoving equipment dangerously idle, threatening a financial tremor that could destroy him.

Returning to Salisbury gaunt and drawn, my father no longer came home to Bien Donné for lunch and began to remain in the office until late at night. Dave Lawley, his managing director, rang our doorbell more and more often, stacks of papers under his arm, and my father would murmur to him, frowning deeply, creating little worried paths in his hair.

His old insomnia crept back, malignant and spreading. He tried hard to relax. Sometimes he rode his bike down to meet me on Saturday mornings after my ballet lesson, and we rode back together in thoughtful silence. He started yoga classes and I lay on the plush carpet of his and Gail's bedroom timing headstands, watching him closely while he twisted and turned, consulting the book for him again and again, checking that he had the poses just right.

Often, while Gail and I lay next to the pool together or sat on the couch gossiping, my father disappeared into the workshop he had built at Bien Donné. There he had a wooden workbench with vices and clamps, where he hammered and screwed fixedly with the tools arranged on the wall. Or he worked in our extensive rambling garden. Well, it's probably more accurate to say he *arranged* our extensive rambling garden, wandering the property for hours in a big straw hat to protect the little splotches of skin cancer on his face, snipping at this and pruning at that. He would tilt his head at bushes that maybe should be moved, briefly oblivious to wars and bankers, saying "*Tata lo* one over there" to John and Patrick, the gardeners, who walked behind him, pushing heavy wheelbarrows with shovels and rakes and spades. Sometimes, when we called him for tea, Dad wiped the sweat from his eyes and complained to Gail that John was "a bloody lazy bugger." One morning Gail confided in me that John had just arrived to work staggering and red-eyed on gallons of kaffir beer. "Your father yelled at him to get off our property, told him never to show up drunk again, and then kicked him so hard John almost flew over the fence," Gail reported uncertainly.

After another round of national service, my father came home even more distant and removed. Battling insomnia for months by then, his comments about lack of sleep began to sound increasingly like pleas. Sometimes we persuaded him to play tag with us in the pool, squealing happily again as he chased us with powerful strokes through the water. Occasionally, he and I still had special quiet moments, like when we untangled lights together before Christmas, but overall he seemed to be withdrawing. I worried about him. While we were watching news of the war on TV, he started to fall asleep on the couch curled into a tight fetal position. Gail sat very still with his head in her lap, stroking his forehead long after the news was over. It made me uncomfortable to see them like that, Gail's concern, my father oddly small and weak. When he announced one Sunday that he wanted to come with Gail and me to mass, I was shocked. I'd never seen him pray.

AFTER GAIL AND MY FATHER MARRIED, WE SAW LESS OF OUR mother. I tried not to worry about her too much, though she continued to call the house often, slurring at Sam, our cook, over the phone line. Gail and I would both panic and whisper, "You talk to her; no, you; no, you; no, you," but it was I, tight-throated, who would have to do it in the end because I was the eldest and she was my mother. I far preferred it when Granny Anne had lived with us and *she* took all those calls.

My mother had become a born-again Christian. On "her" Sundays, she would take us with her to loud services where people in the congregation would suddenly be "seized by the holy spirit," close their eyes, throw back their heads, and then spew out long boisterous litanies in tongues. Sometimes three or four people spoke in tongues at the same time, the minister sweating along with them, rocking on his heels in the pulpit, booming "Swee-eet Jee-sus, o-h-h swee-eet Lor-r-r-d!" Then all the tongue-speakers quieted down and the minister's eyes pinged open, surveying the scene carefully. "Raise your hands to heaven, all of you who are ready to accept our sweet Lor-r-d Jee-sus Chr-i-sst into your hearts today!" he boomed. I stared at my feet and tried to look inconspicuous as Mum hissed at me noisily, "Accept the Lord, accept him, accept him!" buoyed by the energy, pushing hard to try to raise one of my wooden arms.

I didn't really like the born-agains but they were adults, and while they seemed crazy they didn't seem as crazy as my mother. Members of her congregation showed up at her flat at all sorts of inconvenient times, doggedly determined, with Bibles tucked under their arms, ready to reform my mother with some impromptu praying and swaying. For a while she even lived with a born-again couple, the Turners, and we would have tea on the Turners' veranda. Mrs. Turner would tilt her head and smile and Mr. Turner would sit straight-backed with the top button on his shirt securely fastened, peppering the conversation with "Thank you, Jesus" until even my mother pulled a face and excused herself, shunting us off to her small room.

Abruptly, my mother left the Turners, and the born-agains stopped visiting. I tried not to imagine what had happened. I knew how my mother had ended relationships in the past. Once, when she worked as a receptionist in a carpet store in town, Sharon, Lauren, and I waited for her to finish up one Saturday morning: making paper-clip chains, stamping with her ink pad, and banging on her typewriter, like we always did at all her different jobs. Just before lunch she disappeared into the storeroom and found a dead mouse in one of the traps. She rolled up its Jell-O–soft body carefully and nestled it into the cheese and ham of her boss's sandwich, putting a lettuce leaf and the other layer of white bread on top like a blanket. "Just wait," she whispered, with a satisfied smirk, "until he takes a bite."

It seemed unnatural to hate your own mother, and I worried that I was being too harsh, but at age eleven I was protective of my little sisters and furious at the way my mother tilted our world whimsically, even gleefully, tossing off all social protocol if it didn't suit her. Once she took us on holiday to Mozambique, while the country was still a Portuguese colony. In those years the Rhodesian war hadn't yet worked itself up into a frenzy, so the roads were relatively safe from ambush and, since this was just before the revolution, Mozambique was safe too. We drove excitedly all the way from Salisbury to Beira, a seaside town, in my mother's wobbly little Anglia. We'd been to Beira before and remembered that it smelled of salt and seaweed and sizzling *peri-peri* prawns at dockside cafés. The beach was white and sandy with waves just rough enough to be fun, and there was an enormous hollowed-out rusted wreck of an old warship solidly aground at one end. Tall palm trees full of monkeys and coconuts hovered over a big concrete-floored concession stand, gritty with beach sand, full of exotic ice creams and sweets. In Beira, grown-ups were always happy and relaxed, with plentiful Portuguese wine, olives, and cashew nuts, exotic foods you rarely saw in Salisbury, and children played long complicated games on the beach, or in the lifts of the Estoril Hotel, just across the road, where everyone seemed to stay.

A day at the beach, the sun dipping behind palms, my sisters and me teetering on a thin pole we made into a balance beam, playing a wild contest of tickle with my mother as we flew down the slide, when suddenly she jerked out of the game, stared momentarily off into the distance, and then fell thrashing onto the sand, like a freshly landed fish in the bottom of a boat. We roared with delight, watching her open mouth scooping up sand and thinking it was part of a new diversion. It was a few seconds before we realized she wasn't playing; then we noticed her white eyes staring, her face covered in sand and spit, her head banging rhythmically into the bottom of the slide. Strangers ran up, throwing their weight onto her thrashing limbs. I grabbed Lauren's hand, and with Sharon crowding close the three of us deflated into the shadows of the playground, our chests and throats shrinking into tight painful knots.

One of the men who came running toward our mother sort

of adopted us. Tom Davidson was a Rhodesian, camping in Beira with his wife and two daughters, one of whom was epileptic. They later came to visit us once in our room at the Estoril, and I witnessed Mr. Davidson expertly handle his young daughter as, just as my mother had, she gazed wide-eyed for a second before rolling off the bed and gyrating wildly on the floor. I wanted him close by. I continued to suggest visits to the Davidsons' campsite to sit on their low canvas stools around the fire, but they made my mother feel cramped and itchy. At the end of the holiday the Davidsons insisted, to which she only reluctantly agreed "for the children's sake," that they follow us on the long drive back to Salisbury. But once we were out of Beira by only a couple of miles, Mum darted into a side road, turned the car around, and we waited there with the engine idling, our little car seeming to crouch under a tall, flat tree. "What are we doing?" I whispered.

"Shhh," she replied, concentrating. Sharon and I glanced at each other. Lauren, perhaps six or seven, paused in her task of digging through a family-size packet of salt and vinegar chips long enough to look around at the long dry grass with grease and crumbs all over her face. Insects shrieked. The sun pounded. "Mummy, I'm hot," Lauren started to whine. My mother ignored her, staring fixedly at the pale gray road ahead. Soon we heard their pickup and then saw all four Davidsons crammed into the front of the cab, craning to spot us on the road ahead of them, their camping gear piled into the flatbed under a whipping tarpaulin. I glanced quickly at my mother, who broke into a wide and satisfied grin as they went sailing past.

I began to dread leaving Bien Donné, with its dinner parties and laughing, assured grown-ups on Saturday nights, and slow breakfasts on lazy Sundays with the veranda doors wide open and music crooning out of the speakers next to the pool. But every second weekend Sharon, Lauren, and I had to visit our mother for a dingy two days of cigarette smoke and extra-strong peppermints. My mother never rang the doorbell on Friday evenings, perhaps still intimidated by the bitter resolve with which my father began divorce proceedings those few years before. Bewildered by the mysteries of mental illness, he had long believed her tearful excuses about the summonses for stealing and empty gin bottles in her underwear drawer until, one day, something trusting in him broke completely. Suddenly he understood her puzzling behavior as simply willful betrayal and deceit. Angrier with himself than with her, the mere thought of my mother now seemed to provoke infuriating reminders that he had been nothing more than a fool. So he unflinchingly cut her out of his life pretending, as much as he could, that she never existed at all. On weekends, Sam would notice her waiting on the driveway and call us to go outside, at which point she'd get out of her car quickly to touch each of us carefully. "Hello, my darlings," and "I missed you, my babies," she would say, a hazy kind of love, or need, flickering oddly in her eyes.

One Saturday she took us to a diving competition at the Les Brown, the big whites-only public pool in Salisbury, where she often embarrassed us by climbing clumsily over the locked gate that led to the ten-meter board, yelling and waving for us to look as she mounted it before quickly leaping into the pool with a noisy, impossible-to-miss whoop.

She had given us some money that day to buy sweets and a Coke at the kiosk before the contest and, after we had chosen between flat licorice or sherbet, marshmallow fish or gob-stoppers, Mum said, "Let's sit there," pointing at the covered bleachers, which were already packed.

"They're full," I replied, squinting up into the shade to make sure.

"No, no, plenty of room," she said, grabbing Lauren by the hand. "S'cuse me, s'cuse me," she murmured to spectators as she strode on jackets and skirts, her sharp angled handbag swinging at heads, as she pushed her way to the top. Sharon and I reluctantly followed, trying to keep Coke from slosh-ing out of our cups. Looking a little wobbly on her feet, my mother let go of Lauren's hand, it seemed, to balance herself.

"Is this a good spot?" I shouted up at her hopefully.

"No," she panted, without looking back.

A voice came over the loudspeakers. "Welcome to the Les Brown," it boomed. "This is our tenth annual diving championships. . . ."

We had finally reached the uppermost bleacher. "There's a place in the middle!" she shouted above the announcer, as we pushed past knees and stepped over packages and tried to ig-nore the grumbling of people who were craning to see past us.

I suppose I expected her to fall, but I didn't anticipate the horror of it as she suddenly tripped and then crashed down, tumbling over and over, knocking into people, who screamed and tried to protect themselves while she hollered and thun-dered before smacking silent onto flat concrete. She continued to roll, seemingly directly into the pool, only to be stopped six inches from the edge by the solid pole of a floodlight, which she hit with a horrifying thud.

My mother lay there, apparently unconscious, her skirt over her head and her legs spread-eagled. Spectators stood to stare and gasp. Divers and judges rushed forward to check her breathing and feel for broken bones. After a few minutes of urgent conference, they helped her to her feet and gently lowered her into one of the press chairs, while the audience whistled and hooted and clapped.

Finally, everyone sighed and settled him- or herself again. The thrill of shared terror and excitement had bound the crowd palpably closer, and they murmured between themselves now. I heard someone giggle nervously to the stranger beside her, "I thought that was going to be a dive."

Irrefutably exiled from those intimate arbiters of "normal," Sharon, Lauren, and I spun separately, in a barren place of our own, beyond all hope.

LATE SUNDAY AFTERNOONS, WHEN OUR FATHER EVENTUALLY AR-rived to pick us up, I usually felt as though I'd been through a war myself. I would grab my already-packed bag and hurry to the safe red leather of his car interior to wait for him and my sisters there. Soon after, Sharon would follow me, straggling behind with underpants and flip-flops falling out of her suitcase, complaining, "Wait, man, Wend." She flounced in next to me. "Why do you always have to be in such a hurry, hey?"

And then we'd wait anxiously until Lauren emerged.

Every Sunday night Lauren hid—in the corners with the dust, under beds with the gin bottles, in the cupboards with the peppermints. I think my mother enjoyed it, delaying us there. I think she still dreamed she could enchant my father with her dark hair and throaty laugh, so she leaned against the wall, hips tilted, eyes glittering, mouth pouting, while he silently searched the flat, his lips drawn in rage until he would eventually find Lauren and pull her out, hissing and biting like a small animal.

One Friday, Gail and I were alarmed to come home to Bien Donné in the early afternoon and find my mother already parked at an odd angle in the driveway. Apprehensively, we approached the car and saw her body collapsed against the side window. Gail, fretful and fluttering, got Sam to help her and between them they lifted my mother out, Gail rattling off hostess niceties while Mum, thick-tongued and unintelligible, stumbled into the house, bringing them both with her.

After propping her onto the sofa and leaving a glass of water on a coaster close by, Sam abruptly caught himself gawking at a white woman hopelessly drunk and rushed back to his duties in the kitchen. Gail politely excused herself to my mother's slack-jawed expression and hurried to the phone to frantically dial my father on the golf course. Sharon, Lauren, and I held back, silent and wide-eyed, hoping the grownups would be able to fix it.

Not able to reach Dad, Gail came back and perched uncomfortably on the edge of a chair, chatting, trying to pretend that nothing was wrong. The clock ticked slowly. Gail was excruciatingly uncomfortable. After almost an hour, she couldn't bear it any longer and suddenly decided that my mother had sobered up enough. "Well, it's been lovely seeing you, Joan," she said, politely standing, nervously smoothing down the creases in her jeans.

"My children . . . ," my mother slurred.

"I think they're packed," Gail said. "Girls?"

We picked up our bags and Gail supported my mother, walking her slowly, holding her firmly by the upper arm. Sharon's face was pale, her blue eyes wide and unblinking. Lauren, only six, slipped her hand into mine. I dejectedly helped them both climb into the backseat and hadn't quite closed my car door before my mother dropped a heavy foot on the accelerator and crashed into a wall in front of her. Gail had long since hurried away. Trying to yank the car into reverse, my mother began to grate the gears loudly. I leaped out and ran inside, my heart beating painfully as I watched from the upstairs hall window: Sharon's and Lauren's heads jerking as my mother revved the engine, gnashing her car forward and back, forward and back, grinding it around slowly until, with the hood aimed at our gate, she stamped her foot down flat again, and as spinning wheels arched up showers of blond sand, the car launched out of our driveway. I cried, knowing from that moment that I never wanted to see my mother again.

5

No one but Velia, my uncle Donald's wife, publicly said my father's accident was suicide. She confided it to other Salisbury wives in the aerobics class she taught on the lawn of her house, under the heavy avocado tree, creating a bit of a family ruckus and flap.

But everyone suspected it, even me. Hours after I had learned of his death, I went quietly looking for clues, even cornering our nanny, Nelly. "Why are my father's shirts in the bathtub?" I demanded suspiciously. I was certain they were keeping something from me.

"Sorry—I'm so late with the washing today," Nelly replied, a little guiltily, and I felt abruptly chastened for even imagining that there could be more to the story than I'd been told.

I can say, categorically, that my father would never have

Dad.

consciously killed himself; he loved his family too much. But I do sometimes wonder if he was completely in his right mind at the time of his death. All those dark months before the accident, he barely slept. He would come home from work dully, eat a grown-up dinner with Gail, and then collapse, sleeping only for brief moments in front of the TV. Later, once in bed, his mind possessed him, churning up cruelly, in place of relief, images of strangers and friends, business associates and relatives, all losing their life savings because of him.

The last day he was alive I heard him pacing outside, long before it was light, his distant crunching footsteps marking a rhythmic baseline to the throaty *coo-coo* of mourning doves. Minutes later, Shiobhan, still two, who had climbed into my bed during the night, peered over my shoulder and whispered that someone was in the doorway. Too sleepy and a little too nervous to look, I shushed her.

Later that day my father hit an anti-land-mine vehicle head on, swerving, they said, to avoid a messenger on a scooter. The army vehicle into which he crashed had its wheels filled with water. I don't know exactly why they used to do that— to make the vehicle more immovable, more of a force if something hit it? Would he have survived if the tires had been filled with air?

Gail's older sister, Paddy, and her husband, George, carried the news into the dentist's office, where Gail, flat on a wavy black chair, lay with her hands resting on the fluttering baby in her belly. Gail struggled to sit, weighted oddly with the baby, slipping on the chair, metal medical tools clattering.

Sharon, Lauren, and I had gone to town that morning to spend Sharon's birthday gift voucher at Kingstons, a bookstore on Stanley Avenue. I had convinced Sharon, with an older sister's weighty logic, that it would only really be fair if we got something for everybody, even Jack, Gail's loudly deaf and gap-toothed father who, lost after his wife's death, had recently moved in with us. "I'll sell your cars for free," Jack had gratefully promised my dad. "We'll start again, my boy," he encouraged him, slapping my father heartily on the back.

With so many people now at home to buy for, Sharon, Lauren, and I took a long time making our choices. A *Fair Lady* for Gail, a *Reader's Digest* for Jack, a *Time* magazine for my dad, and a magazine about Donny Osmond for me and Lauren to share. Sharon ended up with an *Archie* comic. We didn't buy Shiobhan anything, thinking she wouldn't notice.

When we had finished we went to Union Car Sales, one of my father's used-car lots in town, and asked for a driver there to give us a lift home. "Hello, missus Wendy, missus Sharon, missus Lauren," Robson said, smiling, clapping his hands together and bobbing at each of us, which is polite in Africa. He opened the door of a little Renault so we could climb in, put on his cap, and turned carefully into the traffic. We passed army trucks packed with Rhodesia Security Forces clutching FN rifles, and we waved at them encouragingly. The trucks gave two toots on their horns, and most of the troops waved back. It was 1975 and Salisbury—actually, the whole of Rhodesia—was full of men in short haircuts and camouflage, rumbling and pounding with the energy of war.

We spread our purchases on our laps and continued to argue in the car. "Doesn't Dad already get *Time* magazine?" Sharon wondered, shifting around piles. "Maybe we should give *him* the *Reader's Digest.*" We passed Highlands Junior School, Lauren's school now, deserted for the holidays. Black groundskeepers were painting fresh lines on the tennis courts and cleaning the windows of hostels that accommodated the white farmers' children who boarded during the term. Robson shifted gears to make it up Orange Grove Drive. There was an elderly African on a bicycle straining up that hill that Sharon, Lauren, and I were so familiar with, but we barely noticed him, unlike when we were riding our own bikes home from ballet or piano, when we certainly noticed Africans on the road and pedaled past them quickly. "No, no, this is how we'll do it," I said, shuffling the magazines back to how they were before.

We were puzzled to find so many cars parked on our driveway. Uncle George greeted us with a taut plastic smile and shepherded us quickly up the stairs. As we passed the living room, I glimpsed Gail crumpled into a chair with her neck bent—there were people patting her hands and stroking her head, their voices urgent and soft. As George pushed us through, they glanced up briefly and then hurriedly looked down.

I understood that something was dreadfully wrong and began to weep. "I'm sorry," Shirley, one of Gail's sisters, murmured as she embraced me. I pulled away and stared at her hard.

"Why?"

"Y-your father's . . . accident . . . ," she stammered, confused. My legs buckled and my throat clenched.

"Where is he?" I mouthed, and when Shirley gripped my shoulders I twisted my head painfully away, thinking that if I couldn't see her eyes then this moment wouldn't happen. But the truth had already enveloped me. I knew he was dead.

At fifteen, I was, they said, the only child old enough to go to the funeral. I watched the whole proceedings scared and self-conscious, teetering on the too-high heels my older cousin, Kathy, had lent me, trying to be a grown-up. I couldn't bear to think of my father's dead body, so I worried instead that my carefully painted nails had dried with unattractive air bubbles. Gail put her arms around the closed lid of the white coffin she had chosen and sobbed, her cheek on the hard lacquer, her pale cardigan dropping unnoticed onto the dust, the thorns of scarlet roses pressed into the streaks of black mascara on her face.

At Warren Hills, the crematorium, the priest spoke in soothing tones and chanted while he swung his censer, clanging out heady clouds of incense. Rudely jerking into preparedness, the mechanism holding my father's coffin began to crank awkwardly down into the flames and I screamed, knocking down hymnbooks and shoving as I tried to get out of my pew. Jack grabbed me, urgently comforting, puzzled perhaps at my noisy outburst. No one had warned me that my father's coffin would move, and for one brief moment I had imagined he was alive and trying to get out.

In the days after the funeral, Gail looked up long enough from her pile of wet tissues to say, "I'll take them," her words now like a satin-edged blanket in that terrifying uncertainty that hovered over the question of Joan's children. We asked anxiously if we could call her Mom.

As with politics, Gail had never paid close attention to the masculine world of business and was convinced that my father's relatives and friends, who had passed her milky tea and let her weep on their broad shoulders, would surely be understanding about her new responsibilities and inherited debts. Certainly, in the beginning, Bien Donné was crowded with people, milling, organizing, feeding, and planning. But then, quite suddenly, for any number of reasons, including foreboding rumors about my father's estate and the mundane pull of everyday life, they all drifted away. Auntie Barbara went back to her husband and four children. Uncle Alastair went back to England. Owen, already frustrated with the war and having now lost his best friend and probably his savings as well, immigrated to Australia.

Only thirty, Gail was left alone to support her aging father, a toddler, three stepchildren, and a baby due in five months. She also had a big house with a formal living room, a dining room, a bar, a billiard room, an indoor fountain, a grand pi-ano, a tennis court, and a squash court, where she entombed my father's ashes to keep his presence close. And I shouldn't forget the swimming pool, sauna, and acres of beautifully landscaped garden that would quickly become neglected and overgrown.

Attending her first board meeting at Salisbury Service Sta-tion, wearing flat shoes and a wide-collared polka-dot mater-nity dress, Gail was puzzled, at first, when the men who had once flirted with her so boldly now all avoided her eyes. David Morgan, the lawyer, pulled in his chair and announced my father's estate was declaring bankruptcy, creditors paid out a few cents on the dollar. What's more, the estate was claiming Bien Donné and all household effects on their be-half. "What does that mean?" Gail whispered, horrified, to Uncle Mark, who took his monocle out and rubbed his eyes. "Ian borrowed heavily against his personal guarantee," Mark replied wearily.

"Are we giving up?" she persisted, leaning her face close to his. Mark looked older. Urgent government cabinet meetings now monopolized so much of his time. "But how will I care for five children!" Gail demanded as the men in suits shifted uncomfortably in their seats.

"Creditors want their money," someone mumbled.

"Which creditors?" she asked, swallowing her tears, and David Morgan sighed and pushed a file across the table in her direction. Gail paged through it slowly, overwhelmed with a profound sense of betrayal as she read the names of my father's relatives and business associates and old buddies, who had all whistled when she wore her white lace cat suit and patted her shoulder so sincerely after he died.

GAIL FOLDED INWARD, BECOMING BITTER AND DEFENSIVE. SHE discouraged visitors, even pulling us into the bathroom to hide when Auntie Barbara's car sometimes appeared on the driveway or when our doorbell occasionally rang. Sharon and I left Arundel, the posh private girls' school with its pink walls that my father had driven us to in his white Mercedes every morning and enrolled at Oriel Girls, a government school four miles away to which we rode our bicycles until they were stolen, after which we walked. We gave up ballet and piano and elocution. Sharon sold old clothes to the remaining servants and hopefully bought bottles of Mazoe orange juice, which she kept at the bottom of her closet to offer friends in the unlikely event they were allowed to call. Lauren, only nine, retreated so far into herself that it was almost as if she disappeared entirely. No more music was played over our fancy stereo system. If I put a record on, Gail cried and told me to take it off.

In the months that followed, Gail's sister Paddy was the only one to brave the eddy of swirling emotions at Bien Donné. She helped us make lists of cutlery, photographs, irons, pots, pans— all the household things claimed by my father's estate. They even wanted his tennis racquet, golf shirts, shoes, and ties.

One Sunday, while her husband, George, was away on

army call-up duty, Paddy came over to keep us company and to supervise a lunch of roast beef like we used to have. Sam made his Yorkshire pudding and gravy and carried in a huge salad, roast potatoes, peas, and carrots. Gail sat at the head of the table, wan and listless; Paddy sat next to her, helping with Shiobhan. Their father, Jack, too deaf for formalities, had already started chewing when Sharon eagerly pulled up her chair, cracking its leg loudly. Gail glared at her bitterly, then dropped her forehead onto her plate and sobbed. "Sorry, Mom, sorry, Mom," Sharon repeated anxiously.

Gail suddenly looked up from her plate and shrieked, "They can take it!" She strode over to where Sharon was sitting, pulled the chair out from under her, raised it over her head, and threw it, crashing and splintering, out of the dining room door. Shiobhan started to cry. "They can have it all!" Gail screamed, grabbing fistfuls of peas and carrots and hurling them against the walls. "Everything!" she yelled more loudly, snatching at potatoes and Yorkshire pudding, slices of beef, salad, bread—

"Gail!" Paddy shouted, trying to restrain her. "Gail, stop it!" She grabbed Gail's arms and held on to them tightly as Gail struggled against her, weeping and shuddering. Sharon, scrambling from where she had fallen, was sniffling against the wall. Shiobhan wailed loudly in her high chair. Lauren and I didn't move from our seats.

In fact, the executors of my father's estate did not take Bien Donné immediately. Gail was stubborn about holding on to our house, a place with such strong memories of my father. She managed to negotiate with the lawyers, crying and pleading that we live there incrementally longer; they in turn would sighingly dole out weeks and months to us, and we jerked along for what would become years, never quite getting into gear, much like the way my mother drove when she was drunk.

A SHORT WHILE AFTER I STOPPED SEEING MY MOTHER, SHARON stopped too, and then, finally, even Lauren didn't want to visit her. But now my mother began to phone the house even more often. Gail continued to send her alimony checks, partially out of pity, mostly because my mother made Gail nervous. "Why don't you see her just once," Gail encouraged us. "She *is* your mother," she went on persuasively. "I think it might be comforting for you to visit her now, since your dad. . . ."

I hadn't seen my mother for three years by then, and her flat was far smokier than it had been before. She still had the two antique wardrobes that hid empty half jacks of gin, and the familiar pristine drinks trolley neatly laid out for guests who never came. Covering the table was the same embroidered cloth I used to trace over and over with my fingertips, studying its stale patterns to the beat of the tan marble clock ticking loudly, patiently wishing away long Sunday afternoons and listening for the sound of my father's car.

My mother had dressed carefully, her hair was sprayed stiff and high that day, but her hands shook so hard when she poured the tea that boiling water, milk, and sugar all splashed into the saucers. Nor was she more successful in getting the

flame of her lighter to make contact with the end of the cigarette. "So," she said, inhaling the word deeply, "do you have
a boyfriend now, Bendy-Wendy?" before her too-loud laugh
disintegrated into a hacking cough. I glared at her in disgust.
Sharon sat on a small stool, looking worried. "Have you been
kissed yet?" my mother cackled on determinedly, before she
abruptly noticed my fury, her darting yellowed eyes instantly
crumpling, blurred with tears. Lauren crept onto the armchair next to her and tentatively patted her knee. Sharon
started weeping softly to herself.

We all waited tensely for the allotted time, until we heard
Gail's horn, the signal to come down. I looked away from my
mother's face, unexpectedly pinned up again by the two corners of a fake smile. I continued to hold myself stiff when she
hugged me goodbye, enveloping me in bony arms. Even her
touch quivered like insanity now, heavy and suffocating,
threatening to drown me completely. I wasn't strong enough
to bear her.

THAT SEPTEMBER, IAN WAS BORN. WHEN PADDY KNOCKED ON MY
bedroom door and told me it was a boy, we cried together,
knowing how much my father had wanted a son. We begged to
see Gail that very night and so, even though we knew children
weren't allowed into the Lady Chancellor, Paddy took Sharon,
Lauren, and me to the hospital and showed us Gail's window.
We pushed each other up to rap on the glass and wave to her,
and Gail laughed happily when she saw us, holding Ian up under his arms—scrawny and deep pink without his blanket, his

wrinkled-up face protesting vigorously, his thin bandy legs kicking out at the warm air with sharp quick jabs.

When Gail brought him home, Sharon, Lauren, and I were even more anxious to fold diapers and offer glasses of cold water while the love around us flickered and rolled fearfully, like clownish pictures in a slot machine. When not feeding or bathing Ian, Gail mostly just lay on the bed. Tentatively, we came to her door, never certain of what we might find. Often she'd motion that we should keep her company and we'd hurry in, gratefully pouring ourselves a cup of tea from the tray or tickling her feet with a smooth, caressing motion that she loved. Other times we'd find her narrow-eyed with lips drawn. "Have you been talking about me?" or "Was that a smirk?" she would demand. *No, no, no!* and we'd shake our heads hard, hastening to reassure her of our love.

It was hard not to feel like the stepdaughters, the ugly sisters, the ones to lose in the woods. Sometimes Gail took her babies out to Paddy's for lunch; she wouldn't arrive back home until after we'd made our long hot walk from school, when the house would be locked, and the servants gone. We sat on the step with our chins in our hands, waiting in the sun for her to sail back, oblivious and unapologetic. "Hi," we'd say eagerly, smiling as if nothing was wrong, carefully docile and obedient, padding along next to her as she unlocked the door.

Gail sometimes whispered that I was just like my father, and I tingled briefly with uncertain love and pride. "You're just like your mother," she'd say to Sharon and Lauren, shaking her head when they asked to invite a friend over or didn't pick up their rooms. *We're not, we're not,* they'd beg, greedy for Gail's closeness too. "You are," she insisted, and I felt their terror. "I don't mean anything bad by it," Gail would add, laughing unreassuringly.

When my mother called, I became more and more determined never to speak to her. I wanted to show Gail I was just as strong and resolute as my father. I fantasized that one day Gail would see I was worthy of being a real daughter, like the ones I'd seen arguing with their mothers in the school parking lot. I wanted to become just as happily careless with Gail, as casual about the words I used, as confident with the expressions that might inadvertently wash onto my face.

Sharon and I sometimes waited at the end of the day to walk home from Oriel Girls together, complaining about the heat, the distance, or gossiping about teachers. We often swam in our pool on baking afternoons and afterward lay on the hot stone border, chatting about this and that. On the rare occasions that we went out, it was usually together.

Lauren was a soft background presence; at inattentive moments she drifted into my consciousness, and I would be hit with gasping emptiness, like a punch. One afternoon, suddenly consumed by guilt over my neglect, I resolved to take responsibility for raising her from scratch. Seizing on what had to be the foundation of all solid upbringings—good table manners— I carried an armful of crockery and cutlery up to my room and summoned her bossily. Lauren was maybe ten then, and I, at sixteen, laid out all my props and started instructing her in their use. "Make sure you always start from the outside in," I said. "This is a fish knife," and I waved it at her. "Always tip your soup bowl *outward*," I warned. "Your pudding bowl goes *inward*," and I glanced up to see if she was paying attention, which she was. In fact, she looked so attentive that I was suddenly frightened; I glimpsed desperation in her eyes and knew immediately that I didn't have enough to give. I needed every shred of energy I had to hover around Gail, tickling her feet, working hard to make her forget I was a *stepchild*.

All three of us were obsessed with staying on Gail's bed, possessive of our spots, jealous and wary, even of one another. It was clear I was her favorite. When Gail shrieked how she couldn't cope, or punished one of us with long loveless days of silence, or screamed how angry she was to be burdened with extra children . . . and how much simpler it would be to send someone to Emerald Hill and be done with her altogether, that person usually wasn't me.

Emerald Hill was a brown brick building on a dusty lump of land that had nothing whatsoever to do with anything over the rainbow. It was the orphanage, where lonely white children could be seen walking cautiously, wearing nubby cardigans pulled tightly across their hearts.

Sometimes we drove to Emerald Hill on a Friday evening to pick up an orphan for the weekend. "But why?" I used to complain.

"Because we have a beautiful house, which we won't have for long, and we should share it. These children have nothing at all." Gail replied, concentrating on the road.

"Maybe terrorists shot their mums and dads," Sharon suggested. There were constant conversations at school about friends and relatives killed, but I didn't want to feel sympathetic toward anyone at Emerald Hill, so I glared at her; I knew Sharon didn't like Emerald Hill orphans either.

When we got there, Gail disappeared behind the high brick walls of the orphanage while we waited in the car. Traffic hummed on the busy roads of the suburb below us. A yellowing lawn around the orphanage struggled to live, barbed and matted. Sunbirds flittered, shaking delicate red flowers of thorny aloe clumps. Africans came and went up that long driveway, hitching thin pants secured tightly with belts, kicking up little clouds of dust with peeling-soled shoes.

When Gail finally emerged she would be holding the hand of a small nervous child and talking earnestly to a nun, whose rosary beads swung rhythmically into her skirt as she moved. Sometimes, the sister would hug Gail for long minutes, rubbing her back soothingly in circles, smiling sweetly at Gail's teary face in an it's-all-going-to-be-okay way.

Usually we got a particular girl, a little older than Lauren, named Caroline. She spoke in monosyllables, kept her shoulders hitched to a permanent point halfway up her neck, and had the unhappy disinfectant-and-boiled-vegetable scent of an institution. She would do absolutely nothing, instead staring cautiously with quick darting eyes, spending hours folding and refolding her clothes into smaller and smaller bundles. She didn't even know how to swim. We hated her, this ghost of Christmas future we could become.

One August we took Caroline to the annual Salisbury Agricultural Show, an exciting event where thick sawdusty air held the palpable scent of adrenaline and animal manure. Bikinied girls lured customers to state-of-the-art pool equipment or handed out brochures on the latest in garden furniture. Men with broad chests in RHODESIA IS SUPER or I ZAP GOOKS T-shirts studied exhibitions of Rhodesia's industrial advances or perused special interest rates offered by the Post Office Savings Bank. *Forces Requests*, a radio show for our "boys on the border," was broadcast over loudspeakers as we meandered the grounds: "And a big hi to our favorite RLI troopie, Bill Davies," the perky announcer sang. "We're all missing you stacks and stacks; the beer's already in the fridge, hon; love and kisses from Mum and the kids. Now a special message for Russel Johnson. . . ." She twittered on quickly, with a number of requests to get through.

Most thrilling, though, was Luna Park, the rickety-rides part of the show, with the breath-catching excitement of all its flashing lights, candy floss, popcorn, and organ grinder music. After queuing with Caroline for the Ferris wheel, neither Sharon nor I wanted to ride with her, both of us hissing too loudly, *You go with her; no, you; no, you; no, you!* Exasperated, the oldest and most responsible, I finally went. We spun around and around, high above the show in aloof silence, until I heard choking and a bubbling sound. Caroline had let go of the edges of her cardigan that she always crossed so tightly over her chest and was cupping her hands to catch the thick brown vomit that spewed out of her open mouth in heaving little waves.

INCREASINGLY, GAIL FOUND SOLACE IN HER RELIGION. SOMEtimes she said, "A family that prays together, stays together," and Sharon, Lauren, and I knelt with her eagerly to say the rosary. Of all the attentive Catholic priests who visited Bien Donné in those years, Father Milsch was perhaps the most persistent. He'd invariably arrive just after I'd rushed home from school and put on my new brown string bikini from South Africa. Trying to get a tan, I'd look up and find him smiling at me. He'd crouch down and start a long conversation, spitting slightly through pudgy lips. His black shoes and fat body were forever blocking the last few rays of sun.

Or he would come uninvited into my room when I was doing my homework or writing in my journal, cross-legged on the floor, and give me doughy hugs from behind, his hands enthusiastically clamping and unclamping my breasts. I hated him, so gauche and bumbling, and tried to squirm and wiggle out from under his hands, which I thought had somehow landed on my breasts by an awkward mistake.

Once he opened my bedroom door smoothly, grinning like he always did. I greeted him coolly from my bed without turning off my hair dryer, my arms raised, dryer and brush in hand. He oozed up behind me as usual, stubby fingers working up from my waist to vigorously massage my nipples, but this time his short thick lips stopped to pant wetly on my neck. Moaning and grunting from his throat, one hand blindly patting for my frozen chin, which he must have hoped to be a lever that would twist my mouth around to meet his fat, drooling tongue.

Frightened, I stumbled up. Wiping his saliva off my neck and cheek, I stared at Father Milsch, half panicking that I had made a mistake and offended him, then suddenly hearing Jack's voice bellow from the hall, "Father! Father!" Father

Milsch stood up without glancing at me and straightened his rumpled clothes. As Jack burst through my door with a happy "Father!" Father opened his arms wide, readying himself to give Jack a warm and priestly embrace.

Gail made me confront Father Milsch and I did, hugging my shins into my chest, my words quiet and indistinct behind my knees. He denied it, of course. "Oh, no, how silly. Oh, my, my," he said, slapping his hand to his cheek, convincingly shocked. "What a misunderstanding!" he went on, shaking his head. "I've said mass dozens of times since Tuesday." He sighed and looked smilingly at Gail, saintly and forgiving of the moods and imagination of adolescent girls.

Father Milsch stopped visiting. We didn't talk about him again until Gail mentioned a year or two later that she'd seen him in town with a woman and he had muttered something to her about having left the priesthood.

From Gail's bedroom you could see the whole Colne Valley. It was only a valley relatively speaking, though, since Salisbury itself had been founded on the ancient high plateau that formed most of Rhodesia. Bien Donné was simply built atop even higher land on that already-elevated ground, so that when you looked out the window all you saw before your eyes was treetops skating into the far-off Domboshawa Hills. Of course I knew there were houses and people under those trees, and that if you could gaze past the hills you would see wrecks from land mines and bullet-pitted farmhouses; even beyond that, where the cooler highveld drops off startlingly into barren sun-beaten land was Nyadzonia, in Mozambique, where Rhodesian Security Forces had mowed down hundreds in a surprise attack on a guerrilla (although some claimed refugee) camp. Actually, if you could gaze to the edges of Rhodesia in any direction, you would see bloodshed and hate. But we were isolated at Bien Donné. I knew that Uncle Mark had been to Geneva as part of a Rhodesian delegation to negotiate peace. I'd even heard that one of his many roles there had been as a decoy for Ian Smith, our prime minister: Uncle Mark's shadowy head bobbing in the official limousine, bracing for an assassin's bullet. We were proud of him, even if the Geneva conference had been an abysmal failure, with ZANU and ZAPU nationalist leaders returning home united and more formidable. But we never discussed that at all.

Occasionally, when Gail and I lay on her broad counterpane in the afternoons, we felt our old closeness. Sometimes, she told me how much my parents had loved me, how long they'd waited to conceive me, how the doctor had to pull me out—painfully, for my mother—with forceps, and I'd finger the funny bump on the back of my head to prove it was true.

Gail would encourage me then to be forgiving, to convince me that my mother was suffering from an illness. She reassured me with stories about her own childhood in South Africa—how she had looked like Shirley Temple and used to sing "You Are My Sunshine," how she hid under the bed with her sisters when her mother was drunk. There should be lots of words to describe drunk mothers, like the Inuit have words for snow. *Alcoholic* is too simple; it doesn't begin to cover the enormous variations of fear and neglect.

My mother was a versatile, complicated drunk—a connoisseur of vice. Beautiful, intelligent, and witty when sober, she turned manic when not. She forged prescriptions with pads she pocketed off doctors' desks. She could be found drunk anywhere and at any time of the day or night, and when she was desperate enough she drank methylated spirits soaked through bread to get the purple poison out. But she was never violent.

Gail's mother, Dolly, was more predictable, more distinctly Jekyll and Hyde. Donna Reed during the day, after an evening sipping two sherries in her warm kitchen she'd turn into a monster.

Gail grew up in Port Elizabeth, an industrial city in South Africa not remembered for its beauty. Dolly was a German Protestant, and she and her sisters performed in an all-girls band that played in the local clubs and dance halls in the thirties. Jack, Gail's father, was Irish Catholic, the handsome and spoiled youngest son of a snooty family who branded Dolly "common" and unworthy of their darling son.

Jack was proud of his beautiful wife, who played seven instruments and danced like Ginger Rogers, but he was also jealous and kept her safely at home where there was no dancing and no music. Dolly quickly had five children, Gail being the fourth, and she loyally brought them up as good Catholics, walking them across town to mass every Sunday because they couldn't afford a car, squaring her shoulders proudly when Jack's family drove past without offering them a lift.

In the beginning Dolly was content at home. She drew, painted, hand-smocked her children's clothes, and made stuffed toys for them. She baked and minutely decorated little cupcakes for their birthday parties. But when Jack went away to fight in World War II, she started playing cards with Auntie Joey, the next-door neighbor, to pass the time, and would always share a sherry or two just for fun.

She continued to drink, even after Jack came home from the war. Gail, by this time five or six, would hear her mother preparing dinner, the soft suck of the refrigerator door opening and closing, the clatter of pans on the stove. Then softly, underneath it all, came the sound of the top cupboard squeaking open and the clink of a narrow-waisted sherry glass. It only took a few before Dolly's voice rose and furniture crashed. Jack's footsteps would then angrily crunch the gravel outside, a car door slamming, an engine revving loudly, the children alone with a madwoman.

It was all right, Gail said with a trembling chin, if they stayed out of her way. She and her siblings hid under the bed while their mother strode through the house, taking the windows off their hinges for air, so she could breathe. But sometimes one of them went out, softly pleading "Stop, Mommy," never learning. Then Dolly tipped, tumbling and falling into the place where her fury was fathomless, sometimes snatching for scissors or an ax but always beating, beating, beating with wide, swinging arcs of her arm until, exhausted, she collapsed, ungainly on the bed.

When Gail and her siblings looked at their father in the morning, hurt questions in their eyes, he abruptly motioned them to stop and pursed his lips into an angry *shhh*. "Loyalty and pride," he said. "Loyalty and pride," to which they obedi-

ently nodded. I stared hard at Gail's face and saw the old ago-
nies of a small child pinned helplessly between nightmare
and appearance. Nothing was more important than pretending that theirs was a movie-star family and all was well. That
was where Gail learned her movie-star smile.

ONE HOT AFTERNOON AFTER SCHOOL I WALKED INTO THE
house. "Wendy," Gail called, her voice brittle and tight. I
walked slowly, breathing lightly, trying to anticipate her, to remember what I could have done.

There in her bedroom she waited, my journal open on her
lap. I started to cry at the sight of that secret piece of me. Gail
spoke my words back to me slowly: my romantic fantasies,
my private dreams. "I hate Gail!" she read, on page after page,
pausing at moments to look at me and narrow her eyes.

When she was done, she closed my journal with a clap and
put it safely under the blouses in her closet. Turning around,
she went down a long list of people who certainly wouldn't
want me before arriving at Ronnie, her brother in Port Elizabeth, who could handle disobedience and might do her a
favor, she said, as she yanked a heavy suitcase from under
the stairs. He was due to visit.

I tried to run away but after a few miles realized that I had
nowhere to go. It had been raining, and I breathed in wet
earth, organic and rich. Cars passed quickly, slapping wipers;
green army lorries shook the road, their wheels crunching
and spitting assertively on damp asphalt; bicycles hurried by
with fast-pedaling Africans hunched over handlebars while

I hovered there, watching, a tight pain in my chest, blood pounding in my head, my feet floating off the ground, suspended in pure emptiness. And when the massive sun started to slide past the msasas on the horizon, and the air caught the soft scent of jasmine and nighttime fires, I slowly walked those miles back to wait outside Gail's bedroom door.

I waited obediently for perhaps a month, desperate to tickle her feet, pour her tea, or make her tasty sandwiches. "I heard Sharon lost her tennis racket; I heard Lauren took one of your South African chocolates," I blurted, starving for any acknowledgment at all, but she barely looked my way. When Ronnie finally came and began packing his car, Gail told me to go to my room and get my bag. Joy, her younger sister, followed, offering to help me, and as we walked together I begged her, choking on my words, to plead with Gail that I might not be sent away. While Joy disappeared to see what she could do, I lay on my bed and wept. Regretting my dreams, I was anxious to shake off all other incriminating parts of myself—shreds of feeling for my mother, fragments of loyalty to Sharon and Lauren. Desperate to be loved, I wanted to squirm free of everything I was. After long agonizing minutes, Joy finally reappeared in my doorway and told me I could stay.

WAR

6

By 1965, when white Rhodesian settlers announced their Unilateral Declaration of Independence, the old British Empire had almost crumbled completely. Britain had already lost India. They had lost Sudan, Ghana, and Malaya. And then Nigeria, Kenya, and Uganda. They had given up the territories that became Zambia and Malawi. But when London pushed Rhodesia to increase its black franchise in the face of what was clearly relentless nationalism, the whites were outraged and defiantly declared their independence. Britain knew it was folly but were battle-weary by then. They slapped their seditious outpost with sanctions and left the unruly settlers to it.

Rhodesia's was the first rebellion against the Crown since the Americans in 1776, and the two hundred thousand or so white Rhodesians were no less proud of themselves. They imagined invincibility, even nobility, in their cause. They imagined they could contain millions of Africans stirred by the passions of decolonization with State of Emergency laws.

Technically, the Rhodesian civil war began just one short year after UDI. Zimbabwean freedom fighters date the beginning of the struggle they named the Second *Chimurenga* (the first was a failed uprising in 1896) from a skirmish with Rhodesian Security Forces near the Chinhoyi Caves in 1966. Although the guerrillas in that particular clash were quickly killed and forgotten, thousands of others had splintered into disorganized political factions by the early seventies. Some left the country for military training, only to return and wander pockets of the Rhodesian countryside with Russian guns and Chinese stick grenades in a barefoot, aimless way. Others murdered isolated white farmers, ambushed their vehicles, and lured other unhappy peasants into the struggle with the promise of freedom and fertile white land.

By the mid-seventies, two major events changed the course of what was, up until then, barely a war. First, the new black government in neighboring Mozambique closed one of only two Rhodesian supply routes from the ocean (the other was through South Africa) and established military camps supporting Zimbabwe's fight for freedom. (Zambia, the other front, had supported anti-Rhodesian military camps for years.) Then ZANLA and ZIPRA (the military wings of the ZANU and ZAPU political parties) temporarily united as the Patriotic Front, the PF. Shortly afterward, the country exploded in bloodshed. The Rhodesian government had the advantage of planes, helicopters, and military know-how; guerrillas had the advantage of numbers and widespread support. Rhodesians went on the offensive, bombing camps in Zambia and Mozambique—"culling," the troopies called it, a term that describes thinning a herd, and thousands were indeed killed. Guerrillas responded with inflammatory attacks throughout the country—rocketing commercial flights, massacring missionaries—all to make their point. Terrified black peasants, whose preoccupation had been mostly just surviving off their dry land, were caught in the middle, accused as spies both by government troops, who thought nothing of killing them, and by black guerrilla factions, who would go to whatever lengths necessary to jockey for influence. Hundreds of innocent men, women, and children were burned, raped, tortured, and murdered. It was undoubtedly they who bore the greatest brunt of that devastating and wasteful war.

As a white girl in my relatively safe suburb of Salisbury, I was barely aware of any of it. At seventeen, I nagged Gail to let me quit high school two days before the beginning of my A-level year. I only needed that last diploma if I was thinking of university overseas, and I argued we didn't have the money anyway. Besides, even boys weren't going to university much in 1977; if they were, they weren't talking about it. Leaving the country then was called "taking the gap" and smacked shamefully of cowardice and betrayal.

Chatter in the high school hallways was about Rhodesian army divisions. The Special Air Service, our own squadron of the famous British SAS, was the most prestigious, the football team of the Rhodesian army. The SAS sent eighteen-year-old boys swimming, crawling, or parachuting into Zambia, Tanzania, and Mozambique to "take out" or assassinate rebels or terrorist groups or to lead more elaborate attacks on big camps accommodating hundreds of guerrillas and their families.

Selous Scouts was another prestigious if more mysterious division. Many of the Scouts were "tame terrs," guerrillas who had been captured and persuaded to join the Rhodesian side, but there were at least an equal number of white Scouts too, rugged spies who spoke fluent Shona and painted their faces black. The Scouts' bush-training program was legendary. The joke at parties, which no one would say to a Scout's face, was to remember to flush the toilet because those boys eat anything.

Then there were the pilots and the Grey's Scouts (the mounted division of the army), who were more exotic, sort of like lacrosse or hockey players. Most boys went into the Rhodesian Light Infantry, the RLI. Dating someone from the RLI was perfectly respectable and mainstream—those troopies had reputations for being ferocious fighters—sort of like dating a baseball player. Guard Force boys were responsible for guarding the "protected villages," huge fenced areas that theoretically sequestered peasants from guerrilla intimidation and propaganda but in reality were closer to concentration camps. Dating someone from Guard Force was dubious—sort of like going out with someone from the Ping-Pong team.

Gail agreed to let me leave Oriel Girls. Smiling sadly, she remembered that my father had once dreamed of sending me to a finishing school in Switzerland, where I would've learned how to arrange flowers and speak French; now she ruefully suggested that I learn secretarial skills at Commercial Careers College on Selous Avenue instead. Mrs. Smith, the typing teacher there, was tall and thin with long red nails that tapped furiously when she demonstrated 100 words per minute. In the mornings she stood on a tiny podium, the air tense with anticipation, before shouting "Go!" and clicking her large stopwatch. The room then exploded with a tremendous cacophonous clacking, like a herd of wildebeest on stampede. "Time!" she bellowed, after a minute, and the place dissolved into a sudden disbelieving silence before the low buzzing hum of students counting up their words.

I didn't enjoy it, but then I didn't expect to. I saw working as a secretary or typist as a temporary stage, a dull but necessary step to keep me busy until my wedding day, when I would become a wife and have children and be cocooned in love and closeness. Then my real life would begin.

One afternoon, after I'd been at Commercial Careers for a number of months, I got a message in typing class that my mother was waiting in the office. For a moment I was excited, wondering what Gail could want, before an icy clarity seeped in and I realized that it wasn't Gail waiting for me at all.

I went downstairs slowly, my head so hollow I thought I might faint, pausing on the landing to bend and peer between the rails and through the glass wall of the administrator's office, where I saw that the school secretary had balanced my mother in a chair and was struggling to help her sip a glass of water. My mother wasn't trying to look glamorous. There was no fake smile pinning up her face. I wanted to flutter out of my skin and hide but my body felt like a heavy, dead thing trapping me there, leaving me with no choice but to nudge myself lifelessly forward, continuing down.

When my mother saw me she clumsily pushed the secretary away and struggled to stand. "Wendy, darling," she said, fighting through a haze of thick words, trying to walk toward me, to cling to me again. "I just wanted to see you—to say hello."

I nodded, because I couldn't speak. I pressed my back against the office door while the secretary stared at me with a mixture of pity and horror. I felt quite naked standing there, as if I were revealing some unspeakable shame. My mother paused, supporting herself on the back of the chair, unable to take the few steps that separated her from me. We all breathed noisily like that for a few minutes, the secretary poised, uneasily shifting her eyes quickly between our faces. I stared at the wall beyond my mother. And then I told them both, "I have to get back to class."

As I fumbled with the door, my mother began to weep. "Please," she begged. "Please don't go."

"I'm late," I said, my hand frozen on the handle.

"Please," she said again, as I slowly opened the office door and started to leave.

"Wendy! Wendy!" she called after me. I glanced at her. Only in her forties, she looked seventy. Her hair was dirty and flat on her head. She wore an old orange skinny-rib sweater that emphasized her thin arms, protruding stomach, and yellow skin. Thick polyester pants hung loose on her soft unsupportive legs.

But her face, which had collapsed into hopelessness, was the most horrifying. Her unpinned mouth fell slack and twisted, her wrinkled cheeks were streaked with wet, her yellowed, milky eyes pulled far, far back into her head, a deep gash into her being. I glimpsed the tortured helplessness, a pit of desperation stirred with horrifying love, and then I turned my back and walked away.

TOWARD THE END OF MY YEAR AT SECRETARIAL SCHOOL, Rhodesian Security Forces led by the SAS conducted by far the most ambitious raid of the war to date. Chimoio was another terrorist camp within Mozambique's borders where the Rhodesian army successfully killed more than a thousand.

When I was seventeen, it was difficult, without pictures, to really understand the horror of Rhodesian raids into Mozambique and Zambia. It is only now, with the perspective of years, that I can imagine what it was to gag on the stench of so many dead, or to hear the shattering cries of children burned with napalm, or to feel the terrible sorrow of men and women twisted in anguish, crying in pain, screaming, loose boweled and bloody, as they ran.

As a young woman, I cheered the Rhodesian army's triumphs, remaining unaware. After graduating from secretarial school, I took a typing job at the Rhodesian Consumer Council, a mostly volunteer organization comprised of old ladies, where I concentrated on recording complaints about whether stiletto heels were glued on tightly enough, or the Indian on the corner was putting an adequate amount of beef into his Cornish pasties.

I still lived at Bien Donné. Gail taught that good girls, those who guarded their virginity, never left home too early, and I desperately wanted to be good. I did start dating, though. Boys called or visited me at the Consumer Council. Sometimes at lunchtime I looked out the window and saw them waiting there on Baker Avenue, and I'd hurry down the stairs two at a time, hair flying, glad to escape.

We usually went to Prospector's Bar in the Monomatapa Hotel. A classy popular bar for boys when, at the end of their R & R, they were serious and more sober—a crowded place awash in an uneasy sea of camouflage, packed with troopies thirsty for a last sip of civilization before the boredom and adrenaline of the bush.

No one there spoke directly about their tours of duty. Stickers in the bar—IS YOUR CONVERSATION KILLING?—messages flashed silently on TV—YOUR TONGUE COULD PULL A TRIGGER— or pinned up in ladies' rooms—WOMEN'S LIB, NOT WOMEN'S LIP—had long warned us not to do that. But still, patriotic passion was palpable and I breathed it in eagerly, wanting a family so badly. *Because we're all Rhodesians and we'll fight through thick and thin!* we sang together, arms around one another's shoulders, and I reveled in those moments of knowing exactly who I was: a young Rhodesian girl with sun-kissed shoulders and a Farrah Fawcett hairdo, ready, with my family, to take on any red-eyed Communist who loomed on the hill, not for a minute noticing the cautious black waiters who cleared away our glasses and plates.

I met an SAS boy named Nick at Prospector's and later went to his twenty-first birthday party. We flirted there and he teased me and I whispered giggly secrets to him, my lips softly pausing and breathing on the fine invisible hairs of his ear while I thought of things to say. After he was sent back into the bush, we eagerly wrote each other and made happy plans for his next R & R. But he was blown up while laying a land mine with Gordon, a boy I knew from school.

I learned from Nick's death that when a body has been blown up, they put sand in the coffin to make it feel suitably solemn and weighty. The flesh and bones that really belonged there were in a lonely arid place instead, caught on the barbs of faraway thorn trees, spread and splattered, intermingled with dry grass, rocks, and dust.

After the service, people went to Nick's parents' house in Chisipite to drink and remember him, and I sat close to John, a friend of Nick's from the army. I had met John before, at Prospector's; he had told me there that he used tampons to stuff a gaping wound in his leg, their little strings dangling curiously out from beneath his bandages, like miniature mocking rip cords. "They really do swell to more than twice their size when saturated with blood," he had reported, earnest and impressed.

Irish-tempered, with brown curly hair that he wet to comb straight when he dressed up, John was teased by his mates in SAS about being jowly, but it was more that his face had kind of a square shape; the jowly thing was what Rhodesians called *humor*.

He was decorated for bravery and daring in a squadron where bravery and daring were the norm, but he was so well trained that even after we had dated for years he never admitted what he had done to deserve it. Every time I asked he would shake his head like a snow globe to cloud his memory.

I do know how he got the hole in his leg, though. He parachuted right through the roof of the mess hall at the Kabrit barracks on a training exercise, a six-foot-four-inch two-hundred-pound dandelion tossed in the wind, a loud, rude crashing interruption to lunch, raining blood, flesh, and large flakes of plaster down into the soup.

That night at Nick's parents' house, John and I sat close to each other's raw center. We both felt the weight of the thick African stars and the same stinging in our eyes and emptiness in our chests. We both knew, by then, that survival meant not thinking or feeling too deeply. So we held hands and laughed about how stepping on that land mine must have ruined Nick's whole day.

BANKRUPTCY LAWYERS FINALLY FORCED GAIL AND ME, SHARON and Lauren, Jack, Shiobhan, and Ian to leave Bien Donné, which quite frankly was a relief. The house was mired in my father's memory, a symbol of loss, making it hard for any of us to move on. We rented a builder's spec house on Pippendale Road that was neither too small nor too big and sat, as spec houses do, unsoftened by eager, skinny trees.

Gail was happier after we left Bien Donné. She got off the bed and met Terry, an ex-Rhodesian Olympic diver a little younger than herself who wore pukka beads and the slightly vulnerable demeanor of someone whose wife has recently left him. We all put on our movie-star smiles, and they were married within two months.

Although Gail's rage diminished, it didn't go away. Terry's two children, Tracy and Terry-John, were sullen, bewildered adolescents who would drift into our house, clash with Gail, storm off to their mother, and then float back for yet another round of drama and tears. Little Ian was four by then, a lonely child who seldom played with other children at his nursery school. Shiobhan was six and wrote letters to God:

Dear God,
Please keep our mommies and daddies safe. Help us not drown when we are swimming. Keep us not to be shot when we are in airplanes, and keep the army safe.

Lauren, about thirteen, was no longer that knobby-kneed, spitting child my father had pulled out from under my mother's bed. Having retreated far into the place Sharon called daydreaming, Lauren surprised herself sometimes, I think, as if her own body moved with strings controlled by an unseen puppeteer.

By this time Lauren was quite beautiful. Her hair had grown long, her cheekbones more defined, her eyes liquid and hazel under straight dark brows. Once she shyly came to me and said she had been nominated to represent her year in the Miss Oriel Beauty Competition. Could she borrow something to wear? Would I help her with her makeup? Did I think that maybe, she asked tentatively, I'd like to come and watch?

I did lend her something to wear, but not my best dress. And I might have helped her with her makeup; I don't really recall. I resented the painful pull Lauren had on me, the empty feeling she provoked in my heart, so I didn't go and watch. Only Sharon sat there, surrounded by proud parents, so she could give Lauren a thin hug and say "Well done!" at the end.

SHARON, LIKE ME, WOULD BE TOUCHED BY THE WAR. ONE chilly winter's morning when she was seventeen, Dale, a friend, arrived in his camouflage strangely early to tell Sharon her boyfriend Bruce had been killed on his first week of active duty with the RLI, the Rhodesian Light Infantry. Sharon collapsed and rolled along the length of her closet doors until her body found an opening and fell through it, pulling her teenage clothes down around her, crying and retching among the Mazoe orange juice and belts and dust balls.

Bruce was Sharon's boyfriend more in fancy than reality. He was dark and handsome, and they flirted on the rare occasions she was allowed out. Mostly, they wrote enthusiastically and talked on the phone.

Dale wearily pushed aside the curlers and makeup on Sharon's bed and sat there heavily. He told us Bruce had been part of an RLI team dropped by helicopter into a nearby Tribal Trust Land in order to rescue a farmer's wife who had been kidnapped by guerrillas. TTL's were notoriously treacherous for Rhodesian soldiers. Mosquito-ridden and roadless, their scant muddy rivers made it difficult to find water. The areas that weren't densely treed were overfarmed, tracts punctuated, here and there, by little other than forgotten cornstalks that quivered in a haze of heat and dust. The troopies were barely more than disoriented schoolboys wandering into this new surreal place, where the sun pounded so heavily it was difficult to breathe. When his patrol group stumbled into an ambush, Bruce was shot in the chest and died instantly.

Bruce's funeral was held in the small chapel at St. George's, an old, castlelike Catholic school and Rhodesian landmark that Bruce and Dale had both attended. Allegedly, the white population of Salisbury took shelter there in the 1890s during the first *Chimurenga*, using its turreted tower as a vantage point to gun down black warriors who charged screaming up the hill with their animal skins and spears.

Bruce's RLI mates wore their greens, parade-ground gear, to carry his coffin. They sang "Born Free" from the film of the Joy Adamson story in gruff, tight voices, with no sense of irony at all.

The farmer's wife was released two months after Bruce's death. She tearfully told reporters how, unlocking her security fence for her workers' lunch hour, she noticed three barefoot youths who kidnaped her at gunpoint and then, considerate of her immense weight, pushed her on a bike or in a wheelbarrow two or three hundred miles to Mozambique. She remained in one of the ZANU camps while guerrilla leaders decided what to do with her, until, unable to agree, they finally let her go. "They were very, very good to me," it was later said she admitted.

. . .

BY THE MIDDLE OF 1979, EVERY WHITE MAN IN THE COUNTRY younger than sixty spent up to six months a year on active duty. Thirteen years into the war, two Air Rhodesia commercial flights had been shot down by guerrillas, farmers and their families were murdered daily, Rhodesian Security Forces still attacked camps in neighboring Zambia and Mozambique, and peasants continued to be brutalized by both sides or herded into protected villages.

When he went into the bush, John lent me his purple Datsun, which in 1979 I used constantly. He would simply call me at work when he came back to Salisbury for brief R & Rs and I would pick him up, waiting quietly in the bar at Kabrit for him to finish with the quartermaster, startling boys who struggled by with heavy packs. If they noticed me standing there they gaped, not lustfully but more shocked—as if they had forgotten women existed at all.

John and I always went out with his mates. Sometimes we went to Oasis, a seedy hotel in a seedy part of town where still-jumpy boys sucking hollow-cheeked on their Madisons descended every Saturday morning for shoulder-to-shoulder drinking (more like frantic gulping, actually) and an uneasy scan of who had made it back. It was a place where someone had always vomited in the pool by lunchtime, a few of the bolder girls were topless by early afternoon, and, by evening— if you were silly enough to stay that long—sweaty and harried black waiters had to pick their way through a sea of writhing, foul-mouthed, and foul-smelling humanity.

Sometimes we went up to Kariba, the vast lake Sharon, Lauren, and I had always loved visiting with my father. By the time I was dating John, all drivers wanting to go anywhere outside of Salisbury were supposed to meet at a prearranged time in town and then leave with an armored car leading the convoy, another in the middle, and one at the end. Additionally, most of the hotels and holiday spots around the country had been mortared or rocketed. But none of that made us hesitate. We floated, in a way, on a euphoric only half-sane invincibility that seemed to become more impassioned by undue recklessness and daring. Someone sat at the open car window with an FN rifle, just in case, but we slipped *Meatloaf* onto the tape player and blasted "Bat Out of Hell" so loudly we couldn't dwell on the fact that convoys were often ambushed too. It was quite social, really, traveling with the convoy, automatic rifles at the ready. When everyone stopped to take a mass pee, the girls coyly behind an open car door or a scabby shrub, rugged boys boldly arch-backed, feet wide, thin yellow streams feeding a wide running river, you had an opportunity to linger in the warm sun and chat with old friends you recognized from other cars.

One of the boys' fathers had an enormous and powerful motorboat that could pull "eight-up" water skiing, and we spent easy afternoons drinking beer or cherry plum spiked with cane spirit, untangling ski ropes, and getting antsy when that wait in the murky green water was too long—although crocodiles—*flatdogs*, we called them—seemed a minor worry in the scheme of things. The boys, who had all taken boating and scuba courses with the SAS, took turns driving the boat and, when all eight of us were finally up, would swing a few skiers a little too far into the bay where the cranky hippo lived, just for humor.

After one Kariba trip, John dropped me home late. Gail was sitting up, waiting. "Whore!" she screamed, after I walked in, her nails digging sharply into my forearm as she dragged me down the hall. "Loose slut!" she shrieked, slamming my bedroom door behind us, where she raged at me, her words like hailstones coming too fast and too hard to deflect, pounding on the empty body that remained when my soul had left it, like it always did.

I bought a big trunk, even after Gail whispered later, not looking at me, that she was sorry. Sharon (then seventeen) and Lauren (thirteen) watched silently as I forced the trunk into the backseat of my recently purchased, hopelessly unreliable VW Beetle. Shiobhan and Ian were too little, really, to notice I was gone. I drove to John's older sister, Gillian, who had a small flat in the Avenues.

Gillian suggested I use birth control, something that had never crossed my mind; she even drove me to the bare efficient offices of the Salisbury Family Planning Clinic, where I was handed a gold-backed packet of red pills. I got a new job as secretary at a paper packaging factory in the Industrial Sites and, as the months of 1979 clicked by, the SAS raided Zambia and Mozambique again and again.

By then, on John's R & R, we mostly went to parties where he and his mates simply drank, working hard to keep their memories muted and soft, fluttering far away like moths in numb bodies. Sometimes a sliver of rage cracked through, and a fight would tumble forth into the warm African night. Sometimes they swilled potent and hilarious cocktails from the prosthetic limbs of maimed buddies or soothed each other in their own intimate language about *povo* and *gooks* and *pozzies* and *sitreps*, reassuring themselves there were other people who understood that barren universe where life was meaningless and the only morality was kill or be killed.

If you had asked anyone in the bars or clubs who we were fighting, only the most dull-eyed would have snarled "Kaffirs." Some, more sober, might have said "communism" or "chaos"—the noble terrors the whole world was fighting. Most would have had another swig of beer to avoid the question. In some army divisions, whites and blacks fought alongside one another. Back home, all white soldiers kept their black gardeners and cooks. Some still had adored nannies. Black men and white men sometimes saved each other's lives and called each other "my china" or "my main man." No one in my generation recognized that we were fighting a war to preserve an unsustainable way of life.

Although, to be honest, by the middle of 1979 it didn't seem to matter what we were fighting against. By then, white Rhodesians were peeled raw and had melted together into something base and elemental, a mythic thing pumped with adrenaline and able to soar solely on the thrill of being alive. We were huge, swinging in unison—*Because we're all Rhodesians*—flying high to clutch at the brief ecstasy of too illusive victory and then falling quickly back down, down, down again and crashing into tears.

. . .

I'M NOT SURE THAT PEACE WOULD HAVE COME IN RHODESIA IF IT hadn't been imposed. By late 1979, Nigeria was threatening to nationalize British oil interests unless that government pushed more rigorously for a settlement in Rhodesia. The South Africans, increasingly wary of negative international attention, sensed an opportunity, and suggested the imminent closure of Rhodesia's last supply route through that country. The leaders of Zambia and Mozambique, tired of being attacked, jumped on the bandwagon and began to equivocate about their unconditional support of the nationalist guerrillas. No one fighting was left with much of a choice.

In the last months of 1979, at Lancaster House in London, the men who led white Rhodesia, members of the Patriotic Front (Robert Mugabe and Joshua Nkomo's temporarily united extreme black party), and members of the United African National Council (a more moderate black party) all agreed to a cease-fire. In preparation for an election, Rhodesia temporarily reverted to a.de facto British colony and a governor, Lord Christopher Soames, arrived from England to oversee the laying down of arms and to lead the country through those months of transition.

White Rhodesians were not happy. For fifteen years the government had convinced us we were holding on to civilization itself. We had defied the world, busted sanctions, and were riding high in an exhilarating vortex of terror and revenge; we didn't want a bunch of lily-livered pommies coming in and telling us what to do. We screamed, *Because we're all Rhodesians and we'll fight through thick and thin* even more loudly in the bars, still certain of our nobility and invincibility, still certain that *Rhodesians never die.*

Even after the cease-fire, John spent all his time in the bush. He surprised Gillian and me one night, his camouflage dirty, his face wan in the harsh kitchen light. "We're arranging a convoy of whites into South Africa," he confided urgently. What about my family? I wondered. "You should warn them too," he said, and we sat quietly together for a while, knowing he couldn't give us more details. "You should be ready to go at any time," he finally announced, and then he looked down, trying to think if there was anything more he could add before leaving.

There were many whispered plots in those hazy last days, each of them strumming on Rhodesia's illusions of righteousness. John never told me what the SAS had been scheming or why they had called it off, though I often asked him when he and his friends muttered about betrayal, as everyone did in that time.

The election went ahead. British bobbies poured in by the planeload to guard polling booths all over the country, while we laughed disdainfully at their funny hats and milky manner, not really believing that such soft people could usher in so much change. When the election results were broadcast, everyone at work clustered around radios, shushing tea boys with their rattling trolleys, splashing sugar and hot water unnoticed on desks and papers. Stunned at the paltry support for more moderate black leaders, there was a still and frozen pause before the announcer wearily crackled out that ZANU-PF, Robert Mugabe's faction, had won re-soundingly.

Robert Mugabe had screamed of hanging judges and of bloodthirsty revenge on whites. Women started to cry and then hurried to take their children out of school. Men huddled grimly to shake their heads at the promise of unimaginable chaos; stories filtered in of people packing and driving straight for the South African border.

When I left work that evening I too was scared. I drove cautiously through the Industrial Sites, where a ululating sea of black people seemed to have washed up from nowhere: dancing and chanting, nimbly climbing lampposts and laughing as they nailed up pictures of *jongwes*, strutting cockerels, the ZANU-PF party sign, flapping their elbows, drinking beer, crowing in shimmering twilight dust, hundreds of them, surrounding me.

They say that Lieutenant General Peter Walls, from the Rhodesian army, cabled Margaret Thatcher with advance intelligence, urging her to set aside Mr. Mugabe's victory because of massive countrywide intimidation. But Mrs. Thatcher's comments to the papers in the weeks that followed were both positive and complimentary.

Robert Mugabe appeared on TV that evening, a slim, slightly built man with large heavy-framed glasses. Speaking gently into the microphone, he said, "The wrongs of the past must now stand forgiven and forgotten. . . . If yesterday I fought you as an enemy, today you have become a friend. . . . Is it not folly therefore that in these circumstances anyone should seek to revive the wounds and grievances of the past?"

At midnight on April 17, 1980, the green, gold, red, and black flag of Zimbabwe was raised for the first time. Prince Charles and Indira Gandhi were there. Bob Marley paid for his own ticket out from Kingston. When he sang the first notes of his famous song, "Zimbabwe," frenzied hordes from the nearby townships surged and clamored, screaming and chanting and rattling the gates of the already seething Rufaro Stadium, causing the police to fire tear gas directly into the crowd. Order was only restored when ex-ZANLA guerrillas marched through the area with raised clenched fists. Until I watched the vast ecstatic crowds at the independence ceremonies that night on TV, I'm not sure I had ever understood that the eight million Africans in Rhodesia had really existed.

7

There is a sound to peace, like the eerie quiet after the emergency brake has stopped a runaway train or the heart-clenching stillness that pounds in the moments concluding a nightmare.

Suddenly, there was no National Service, no R & R, no shoulder-to-shoulder drinking at Oasis on Saturday mornings, no gut-wrenching On Government Service brown envelopes holding thick call-up papers, no parties where we felt the terrifying thrill of simply being alive.

Some of the Rhodesian Army divisions switched allegiances to the new Zimbabwe as snappily as an about-face on the parade ground at Cranborne Barracks. John's all-white SAS C squadron, however, was disbanded. The farewell ceremony at Kabrit was quite beautiful, the entire unit leaping from the sky before floating down softly above our heads. But when we got home, John paced angrily, feeling betrayed and confused.

He had spent his life obeying: first at an all-boys' Rhodesian boarding school, where children were bullied into conformity; then in the army, where staying alive meant holding to rigid commands. No one had wanted his opinion for twenty-two years, and then everything abruptly changed, like a revolving stage that flips unexpectedly, and he was abandoned with no direction, stumbling and disoriented in a new and unfathomable world.

Some of his friends became bodyguards in Europe or went north to fight in other wars. Others became darting-eyed casualties of killing, people to treat warily or avoid altogether. John told me he was offered a position by Americans to train Iraqi soldiers against Iranians, but his father begged him not to take it.

His sister and I conferred closely. We smoothed down his hair, handed him wrinkle-proof trousers and a short-sleeved button-down shirt, and pushed him into a salesman's job with UDC, a local finance company that sent him out on red dust roads in a gray Peugeot company car to meet with farmers on their cool cement verandas. There he brushed thick dog hair off farm cushions, balanced thin china teacups in his hand, and sat forward in his seat, offering loans and commiserating about the price of tractors and seed.

The feeling in Salisbury had also changed. Renamed Harare (after one of the townships), it gradually began to take on an African overlay similar to what I'd seen when I played in the *kaya* as a little girl: loud, smoky, sweaty, and communal, with just a faint edge of uncertainty. Maybe only the whites felt the uncertainty, concerned as we suddenly were with tit for tat.

The foreign ambassadors and diplomats in the big houses surrounded themselves with high security fences and brisk guards. Chickens wandered into suburban kitchens, and small crops of maize began to sprout, defiantly and increasingly, in very English gardens. Overstuffed vehicles, seemingly held together with tape and string, began to choke the roads, coughing past dozens of wobbly bicycles, leaving them in dark clouds of diesel. Harare Park became more carnival-like, especially over weekends. Yelling vendors waylaid tourists with their rickety mishmash of stands, people brought their *sadza*, gritty cornmeal porridge, for noisy picnics, and bevies of black brides led parades of happy guests and multitudes of chattering, brightly colored bridesmaids.

In the beginning, the old British colonials muttered snootily about the lack of decorum, but they didn't get rid of their servants. In spite of Zimbabwe's new minimum wage and tougher labor laws, they kept their cooks and nannies and gardeners (who now all held their heads a tad higher). The only difference was that when the houseboy or maid brought the tea in the early morning they had to wait patiently with a heavy tray while their disheveled *baases* and *madams* fumbled sleepily with all the keys for the newly installed wrought-iron interleading doors that separated the more vulnerable bedrooms from the TVs and stereos that *tsotsis*—thugs—now loose in the suburbs might want from the other parts of the house.

The new government kept all the tough old Rhodesian emergency laws and censorship prohibitions carefully in place. Robert Mugabe and his motorcade, consisting of two or three long dark cars peopled with shadows, started driving assertively through Harare's streets.

Etiquette demanded (under pain of being shot) that the world stop reverently when Robert Mugabe drove by, mountains of bicycles and buses and dilapidated vehicles piling up behind one another like elephants in *The Jungle Book*. Borrowdale Road, the large main thoroughfare in front of Mugabe's residence, was closed from 6 P.M. to 6 A.M., but the warning boom that was meant to bar access to the street was rarely lowered. Occasionally, oblivious tourists or drunks were fired at, and one or two I heard were killed.

A couple of years after Independence, there were dark rumors that Mugabe had ordered *gukurahundi*, a massacre of Ndebeles (the tribe from Southern Zimbabwe who made up the majority of the other party in the Patriotic Front during the war). Up to twenty thousand people were starved, tortured, and burned out of their huts, the whispers said. But by then the *Zimbabwe Herald* reporters knew better than to investigate.

JOHN AND I MEANDERED ALONG IN THE NEW HARARE. HE lived with four school and army friends in a big white Rhodesian-style house with a green tin roof in Milton Park that they called the Verge Inn—a place with a shabby garden, a small bright pool off a large room that we had converted into a wide and prominent bar, and two or three servants who cleaned up after the parties, washed dirty towels and underwear left on the bathroom floor, and cooked us big greasy breakfasts on Sundays.

For two years, I practically lived there too. Loving and gentle, John absorbed me into his family. I drank Pimms cocktails with his father, and his sister and I became best friends. We'd spend idle weekends on his uncle's rambling farm, went to his dotty great-aunt's teas, and cheered at his young cousins' rugby and cricket games. They all remembered my birthday, and I had a regular place at the long family table at Christmas.

But still, John was uneasy and out of step with his life: once a shining hero in an anarchic universe, now a drab salesman of interest-rate payment possibilities, living his life in an eight-to-four rut. I sat in the Peugeot waiting for him to drive me to work one April morning, when he slammed his car door so hard that the glass in the window vibrated and paused, momentarily whole, before it suddenly fragmented and collapsed completely into my lap, like the tears he never shed.

Sometime afterward, he left his gray company vehicle and got on a plane bound for Aberdeen, his army SCUBA training having come in handy for diving on oil rigs in the North Sea. He was more familiar with that rhythm, a ruggedly masculine unemotional environment and brief periods of danger interspersed with long hours of boredom. Alone, he gazed at his watery reflection in the silver-studded walls of a decompression chamber, trying to see who he was.

. . .

ALONE TOO, I TOOK A DEEP GULP OF DUSTY AFRICAN AIR. I WAS now a *Zimbabwean* girl. Zim-bab-we-an. It even sounded sweaty and African, like a dirty top-heavy bus, or twangy music on a thumb piano. I tried on different variations—a Zimbo, a 'Babwean—shifting my shoulders, holding my tummy in, looking for something that felt becoming and comfortable.

I was working as a secretary at a cigarette factory, the only woman on the production side, leaving me flattered by lots of attention, the men always taking me out with them on their business lunches where I chatted and flirted, pert and pretty. My job was to type, answer the phone with a cheerful "Mr. Davidson's office," and give tours of the sweet-smelling factory wearing a cute navy and white uniform with the company logo on my blazer. For this, I learned interesting statistics about cigarettes-per-minute and quality control. I explained how the shiny navy and white packaging was for export only while the red and grayish newsprint boxes were for local consumption. I clicked though the factory wearing my navy stilettos and pantyhose, nodding at workers in their dark overalls, striding across the ruddy tobacco-spread floor assertively with my carefully blow-dried hair.

I became friendly with Carol, who worked in the personnel department. She was also ready to find adventure, so I persuaded her, over a number of giggly lunches in the company cafeteria, to take a modeling course with me. The modeling teacher, a well-known Greek woman, Evanthia Paphitis, had won the annual Rhodesian Swinging Miss competition that I had seen live five or six years before. Evanthia had sashayed down the runway in a wide yellow skirt with her dark hair bobbing and her white smile flashing, winking and twirling and doing a little two-step at the end of the ramp. The crowd had gone mad. She answered the host's questions in a witty and confident way, and after she won, her picture was splashed all over the *Rhodesia Herald* with little tidbits about the things she liked and her ambitions.

After seeing her, I was inspired. I wanted to be a Swinging Miss too. Uncle George, Paddy's husband, had a friend, a photographer who once asked me, when I was about seventeen, if I had ever thought about entering Swinging Miss and offered to take the pictures. Although I had thought about it a lot, I just smiled coyly and said in a ladylike way, "I wouldn't mind," as if I had never considered it before and might think about doing him a favor. I daydreamed about pictures of me in the *Rhodesia Herald* in short shorts and a halter top, leaning against a tree pouting, or sitting on a swing with the camera angle a little high to show a bit of cleavage or something. If we did the swing shot my bio could say, "Wendy, a real Swinging Miss! Wendy enjoys swimming and listening to music and one day wants to travel the world. Best of luck to Wendy!"

But Uncle George's friend never mentioned it again, so I never was in the *Rhodesia Herald*. Mr. Davidson did enter me for Secretary of the Week in the *Financial Times*, where a picture and a little blurb about my efficiency and capability appeared, but it wasn't the same. No one I knew read the *Financial Times*, and I never did sashay down a runway and twirl to a roaring crowd like Evanthia.

By the time Carol and I began taking our modeling course with Evanthia, it was too late for Swinging Miss. When the country was still Rhodesia, the competition organizers had managed to restrict the number of black entrants to only three or four girls. Now, with Independence, they weren't allowed to do that, so they scrapped the whole competition, deciding a Swinging Miss with mainly black competitors wasn't really worth it.

Carol and I still practiced our sashaying in my boss's office during our lunch hour. I thought if I became good at it, and confident, I might get modeling jobs over the weekends or be asked to do a television commercial like Debbie in Finance, who sat at a window in her bra with billowing sheer curtains and streaming sunlight, staring vacantly into the distance, putting on deodorant while classical music played in the background.

Sometimes Mr. Davidson came back from his lunch early to watch Carol and me ham it up a bit with our pouting and twirling. Mr. Davidson would tease me affectionately and say that I was doing a great job and he was happy he had hired me. He confessed, chuckling, that he usually only hired women who, when they clasped their hands behind their head and pointed their elbows toward the wall, had breasts large enough to touch the wall first. I grinned broadly, flattered.

I spent very little time visiting home. Gail had had two more children with Terry, her second husband, which gave her four in all—nine if you counted accumulated offspring from both of their previous marriages. Sharon, with stellar results from her final exams at school, decided she wanted to go to university. With the war being over, some of Sharon's friends were going to university now and so, inspired, Sharon arranged a formal meeting with both Uncle Mark and my father's brother, Alastair, bravely asking them to raise whatever funds they could from the meager remains of my father's estate. Both Mark and Alastair looked at her sternly and promised to support her on condition she was absolutely certain university was what she wanted. "Well . . ." Sharon stammered, wishing she could picture more precisely what university might be like. We didn't know anyone who had actually *been*, although Gail had heard rumors of girls who came back ruined. "I'm not *exactly* sure," Sharon told Alastair and Mark, suddenly afraid.

So instead she took a local job managing a suitcase shop on Speke Avenue and left home, moving into a little garden flat with me. Lauren, fourteen, was sent to boarding school in Marondera, about two hours northwest of Harare, where none of us drove to see her on visitors' weekends.

On the quiet Sundays when other girls were busy with their families, Lauren sometimes wrote me in a formal schoolgirl hand—*How are you, Wend? What do you think a friend really is? Should I take art or English? Why do you think I'm no good at math?*—as if she was listening hard for herself, wanting reassurance that she existed at all.

Once, I met her bus when she came in for a half-term weekend. I left work during my lunch hour for the stop near the tobacco auction floors and waited there for her, breathing in dark clouds of burning rubber and sweet tobacco. Black ladies sat on blankets under scant trees swatting flies, nursing babies, doing each other's hair, or laughing in that shoulder-shaking African way. Black men, stripped to the waist, would stare hopefully into hissing car engines. Pie boys—teenagers, really—grinned widely, luring customers, wobbling past on bicycles with too-big trays.

When the school bus spluttered to a stop Lauren smiled shyly, a little uncertain, as though she wanted to make a good impression. Her shapeless uniform was belted tightly at the waist, her short white school socks prim and stark against the pale brown of her dusty leather shoes.

We chatted together on the pavement, sweat prickling in the hot sun while we unloaded tennis rackets and hockey sticks, briefly enjoying the relaxed, shy intimacy of people who know each other well but haven't really talked to for a very long time—it was different being with Lauren when we were both away from home. As we stood there talking, other girls' mothers flew past us with warm smiles and cool drinks, kissing their daughters tenderly on the cheeks, encompassing them with strong protective arms that led them back to their cars. Together, we watched those mothers distractedly, not really noticing that special love anymore or at least pretending not to.

When Lauren was back from school, she lived with Gail and Terry and their children in a new house that had a gurgling swimming pool, a lush lawn, and tree orchids nodding shyly out of the msasas. Elephant ears, ferns, and cycads tumbled lushly out of pots. White petunias grew in chaotic profusion. Scarlet bougainvillea wrapped itself seductively around fever trees. At night, Gail and Terry and their children slept safely behind a big gate, hastily installed at the top of the stairs after Independence. Lauren slept on the other side of that gate, in her vulnerable bedroom, far away.

One Saturday, I arrived to find Lauren crying and Gail spinning tight-lipped in old unreachable fury. Surprised by some rare friends the evening before, and anxious to make a good impression, Lauren had poured her friends a taste of liqueur.

"You will not touch my belongings!" Gail screamed at her now. "You're a thief and a drunk like your mother!" she yelled dizzily, as she grabbed Lauren's ear, dragging her violently across the room.

Lauren's arms flailed wildly, clutching at nothing. "Sorry Mom sorry Mom sorry Mom," she cried through thick saliva, weeping, battling to keep her balance, tripping and stumbling, trying to lift her head, blinking through tears and wet strands of hair, gasping for little snatches of breath as Gail shoved her roughly into her faraway lonely bedroom.

"And don't come out!" Gail bellowed, loudly slamming the door.

I sat very quietly. My throat closed and my chest clenched violently with the feeling, now familiar, that I came to recognize as heartache. When I was younger, I thought you could die from it before I learned that it eased if you let your spirit scurry away, safely, like a small burrowing animal. I was twenty-two. Even then, I was desperate for Gail to love me. Even then, caring for Lauren, protecting her from being hurt—abused, even—was not more important than that.

IT WAS A COOL AND CLEAR EVENING IN MAY WHEN SHARON returned home to the little flat we shared in Avondale, telling

My mother, 1956.

me that she had received a call that our mother was dying in the Pariyenatwa, a big state hospital in Harare.

"Lol and I don't want to go visit her by ourselves," Sharon said. Something cold and heavy was trickling through my veins, and I couldn't answer her. "Please, Wend," Sharon begged.

"I can't," I told her, my voice echoing oddly against the rushing in my head.

So Sharon and Lauren went alone. They walked a long, dimly lit hall to a little room where my mother lay alone. She was staring blankly and breathing ragged air, but when she saw them she tried to sit, her face strangely shrunken and her teeth grotesquely big as she smiled. Sharon and Lauren sat stiffly and, after five minutes, promised to come back, which they did, once or twice. There were never any other visitors.

I stayed far away. I was terrified that if I actually saw my mother I might still see love for me in her eyes, and I was certain I could never stand that.

Gail was very supportive after my mother died. Friendly with the undertaker at Doves Morgan, a funeral parlor off Angwa Street in Harare, she arranged and paid for a ceremony there in the little chapel room with a red carpet, piped music, a podium, and a bouquet of pale arum lilies. There were very few people in attendance, and not one of them offered a eulogy.

After the ceremony, we simply stepped out onto the hot pavement, shading our eyes from the sun, shouting loudly at each other above rattling lorries and honking cars, trying to remember where we were parked. There was no time to ask, What will happen to her body now? although in retrospect I probably knew that she would be cremated and her ashes buried under a small plaque at Warren Hills, outside of Harare, near the newly built Heroes' Acre, the Liberation Struggle Memorial. Sharon took care of emptying her small flat and selling her possessions. I wanted nothing that had belonged to her.

I don't remember Lauren's reaction to my mother's death; she was only sixteen. A few months before, her headmaster had told Gail it was pointless to spend any more money on her education so Lauren had already left school, to move back with Terry and Gail and travel into town every morning to learn secretarial skills, as I had.

Totally adrift by then, she would cover her eyelids with bold-blue imported Christian Dior eyeshadow, but she stared out cautiously from beneath it with no trust for the world at all.

AMERICA

8

When Lauren was seventeen, after she finished secretarial college, she too got a job in the Industrial Sites. Gail drove her around to find a place to live, finally settling on a small flat in Avondale, which she moved into before her first paycheck. After losing a close friend in a train accident, Sharon had spent months comforting the bereaved husband, Butch, and was now slowly falling in love with him. Inexplicably restless, I decided to leave Harare and move to Johannesburg, where Gillian, John's sister, was living. Once again, she invited me to move in with her until I found my feet. I got a job teaching hastily learned aerobics at night and tried to sell advertising space during the day, driving on cold calls to customers, always tearfully lost, having no idea that maps can be useful or that in big cities it helps to pay attention to north, south, east, and west.

Johannesburg was fast-moving and dizzying, with tall build-ings and bright shopping malls. People were different there too: carefully fashionable, obsessed with gold and cars. Even the racism in South Africa was different; sharper and angrier, it lingered malevolently closer to the surface of my con-sciousness.

One chilly winter's evening, Gillian came home and asked me if I was interested in going out to dinner as part of a four-some. An American named Mickey, who had been working with her boyfriend in a shipping chartering company, had just returned from a motorcycle trip through southern and central Africa. "He's a little odd," Gillian warned, but when she saw my face she quickly added, "Come on, it'll be fun; he's not *so* odd, he's more—well, different."

I wanted to be daring in my new life in Johannesburg, but I had no idea what to expect from Mickey. I had never dated a man who hadn't killed someone, or at least been prepared to kill someone. I had only ever met two Americans. One was a female exchange student who tried to start a boisterous cheerleading squad at my fancy private high school; the other was a balding, lumpy man from Texas who had dated Gail and talked in a long slow drawl that we mocked behind his back.

Mickey called and we talked. He flung out wry fragments of humor, like friendly little Frisbees, and I caught them. We made plans to go to dinner with Gillian and her boyfriend at a fashionable French bistro in a suburb close by.

I dressed carefully for the evening, leaving myself at least an hour to fuss with my makeup and nails, as I always did. Mickey, tall and curly-haired, picked me up and we drove alone in his car. On the way there we bantered and chatted, his voice gentle, his accent lyrical. I knew how to handle men by then. I was confident of the routine and had a repertoire of charm that I ladled out just enough of to keep the phone ringing and the weekends less than dull.

Mickey surprised me, though. After the usual chitchat, he casually asked me what I thought of the political situation in South Africa.

I was shocked. No one had ever asked my political opinion before. Actually, I'd always been quite wary of offering any opinion at all. And experience had taught me that politics was a particularly divisive, even dangerous, issue. Those who had disagreed with the Rhodesian government usually left the country, while those who stayed muttered scathingly about the cowards and commies who "took the gap." The few liberal whites remaining in Rhodesia were called kaffir lovers. If you were a woman, "kaffir lover" took on connotations of sexual perversion—even insanity. Not a true white anymore, but not a black.

A nobody.

I told Mickey that I didn't know what I thought.

We were driving past a grimy Greek grocery store. SIMBA CHIPS TASTE GRRRRR-EAT! A faded cartoon lion beckoned, while Africans milled against the dust-splattered wall, talking and laughing. We passed scores of people pedaling bicycles, or walking arm in arm, or beating up grit with rubber flip-flops, parcels, and baskets clutched tightly in their ashy black hands. I was relieved that we were almost in the parking lot of Chez Annette, and could already see Gillian and her boyfriend waiting casually outside, when Mickey said he'd drive me around the block so I had time to think about it. He was curious to hear my answer.

His air of relaxed attention and expectation felt more odd than threatening. I scanned his face for clues, nervous that there might be only one answer in America, like there was in—well, it was called Zimbabwe by then. But I could read nothing in his expression. We drove in silence while I groped and fumbled, a blind person in a new place. Finally, I said that I thought a government could keep a group of people down if they were brutal and deprived them of all hope, but that it was almost impossible to maintain that level of oppression indefinitely. Once a government relaxed its hold, even a little, people would push hard and be impossible to control.

I looked at Mickey hopefully. He nodded without taking his eyes off the road, neither surprised nor offended. He said that was what one of his college textbooks on revolution had said. I felt very pleased with myself.

A few days later Mickey knocked on my door again. He wore a button-down collared shirt with the top few buttons undone and a brightly colored bow tie fastened around his bare neck. He offered to take me to an Italian movie, *The Tree of Wooden Clogs*, which would be the first time I had ever seen a movie with subtitles. Sitting in the back row of the nearly empty theater, Mickey rummaged in his backpack before pulling out a tin cup and an expensive bottle of champagne that he opened with a loudly echoing pop. We giggled, shushing each other in the quiet blackness, and watched the movie, sipping champagne and chatting quietly through the boring parts.

Mickey called again and again. He took me to cramped bohemian restaurants on Rocky Street, where we blinked away smoke, shouting to hear each other. We had fancy dinners at the very top of the Carlton Center, where he laughed at my awe of the lights of Johannesburg, saying I hadn't seen anything yet.

We met in bookstores, and he demonstrated what fun it was to sit on the floor and read for free, and I moved my limbs away, nonchalantly like he did, when people, grumbling, had to step over us. When he collapsed, panting and exhausted, on a crowded dance floor, lying there spread-eagled to save our spots, at first I was horrified; then, suddenly wallowing in devil-may-care, I laughingly lay down too.

Mickey was definitely odd. I had heard that he used to play basketball on a team from Soweto, the African township in Johannesburg, and it was embarrassing to think I could be dating someone who had once fraternized with blacks. I'd also heard that he was Jewish, but he seemed perfectly normal (well, apart from what seemed to be a rebellious spirit), so I decided it would be impolite to ask him about his religion directly. Luckily, I didn't know too many people in Johannesburg who might see us together.

Mesmerized by Mickey's unruly thinking, I was greedy to be with him, so we continued dating and when, after six weeks, he asked me to follow him to Europe, it seemed that the perfect solution was simply not to tell anyone I was leaving and to tell myself that—after a mere few months in

Mickey.

Johannesburg—I was now worldly and sophisticated, coolly embarking on a casual womanly fling.

I did tell Gillian, but I walked away from both my jobs without an explanation, and only at the last minute, unable to quite contain my excitement, did I call Sharon and Lauren. Now that we were no longer at home, vying for Gail's attention, Sharon, Lauren, and I had relaxed into becoming closer. In fact, living at a safe distance in Johannesburg, I had recently embraced a clucky, rather maternal role with my younger sisters and called them often to offer newly urbane advice. When I confided my travel plans to Sharon, she said, "Who is he again? What are you doing? When are you back?" making me repeat the details of my trip over and over, her voice squeaky with concern, while I chuckled at my own audacity. When I called Lauren, she said, "Oh, that's nice, Wend," and nothing else.

"How have you been, Lol?" I prompted.

"Fine," she replied, and then, "Did I tell you I woke up and found a strange man in my flat the other night?"

"A man?"

"I woke up hearing a noise and there he was, pulling my clothes out of drawers."

"No!"

"I screamed, and then he looked so frightened I quickly jabbed my finger in his back and marched him out the front door."

"And then?" I demanded. There was a confused pause for a moment, as if she was wondering what I could possibly mean.

"Well," she said slowly, trying to remember, "I put my stuff away and went to sleep."

"But didn't you call someone?" I almost shouted at her. There was another pause.

"Who?"

I didn't know. The police in Harare had no transportation and needed to be picked up. Neither Sharon nor Lauren had a car. She knew no one in her block of flats.

Suddenly I felt as though I were struggling to hold Lauren up. All that separated us was a thin membrane that permitted vulnerability to flutter through; I thought I would choke.

So I hurriedly said goodbye. I squeezed my eyes together, forcing Lauren and her terrifying loneliness far out of my mind, then eagerly got on a plane with Mickey to leave Africa completely.

. . .

MICKEY AND I FLEW TO ROME, WHERE WE WALKED THE CITY
and slept in dim-lit pensions. We traveled in third-class com-
partments of overnight trains north through Florence and on
to Venice. Then we moved on toward Austria and finally
crossed the border into the little towns of Switzerland.

On the Spanish Steps in Rome we discussed politics. We
listened to Handel in churches in Kitzbühel. We went to art
museums in Florence where he told me what he knew of art
and shrugged his shoulders at what he didn't.

I loved his boldness, how he danced on the Rialto Bridge
and smilingly offered to take pictures of tourists before they
asked him. I loved how he engaged strangers in conversation
or, judging a line too long, held my wrist to sneak through the
exit, so we'd see an exhibit backward, paying at the end. I
loved how the minute we got to a new place he would go for
a run and come back breathless and excited, urging me to get
ready quickly, pacing with possibility.

I studied the way he moved, lithe and loose-limbed, a small
smile playing constantly about his mouth. And how he wore a
bandanna and swung a backpack and threw his head back to
gulp water from a big bottle on humid, sweaty days. He closed
doors softly if he thought I might be sleeping, he elbowed
away people he thought might push, he touched me with gentle fingers as if I were something precious that might break.

Mostly, though, I loved how he spoke to me. We leaned
close across tables to hear each other. Mickey fascinated me
by the things he knew and the way he asked questions,

marshaling his thoughts, looking around for words as if they hung somewhere in the air. When I answered him, he would look at me so intently it felt that even the spaces in between my words held meaning. Mickey could tease thoughts out of a person and make her feel like she knew something. What he saw in me I had never seen myself.

After three weeks, it was time to say goodbye. Mickey asked whether I was ready to go back to South Africa; I said no, still elated by a breath-catching power I couldn't define but didn't want to lose. So we went to the American embassy in Switzerland, got a visa for me, and boarded a plane bound for John F. Kennedy Airport in New York.

I was so excited to see America. Leaving the airport terminal, I laughed in delight at real yellow cabs and the loud accents I had only heard on TV. Warm air through the bus windows tasted salty and damp and smelled of gasoline; the light was misty and soft. I was shocked at the disheveled highway, enormous cars bouncing with extravagant suspension over cracks and potholes, trash fluttering on embankments; as we crossed the Triborough Bridge, Mickey pointed out Manhattan, a place painted confidently on the skyline in gray concrete strokes. I could only nod, hardly believing I was there.

Mickey's mother, Livia, met us at the Yonkers bus depot. She had only arrived in New York herself a few decades before; she and her Hungarian mother had come straight out of a German displaced persons' camp at the end of World War II. After clearing immigration at Ellis Island, they made it no farther than Queens, where they would meet other Jewish refugees and start to rebuild their lives.

Walter, Mickey's father, a young German immigrant, was the beloved son in a family of those other European Jews. Both Livia and Walter were more than ready for the fifties sirens that sang of happiness and the elusive American dream waiting in the suburbs, so they married, bought a little house in Yonkers, and had two children, first a girl and then a boy. Walter joined a New York trading company and threw himself behind a career; let those German schoolyard bullies just try to touch him now.

Mickey's parents stayed together for almost twenty years, until Jackie, Mickey's sister, went to college and Walter, a hard-hitting American trader by then, decided that he really had little in common with Livia after all, so he moved into a penthouse on Central Park West, leaving Mickey and his mother suddenly alone.

When Livia pulled up to the steamy Yonkers bus stop that morning, she sprang from the car to help us with our few bags, chatting excitedly in her funny Hungarian accent as I sat quietly in the back looking out the car window. I hadn't had much experience of scruffy suburbs with overflowing garbage cans. I had never seen unshaven white men publicly idling in their undershirts, or black teenage boys striding widely with a level gaze. Both seemed a little dangerous.

Livia waited for Mickey to tell her where to drop me off and, when he didn't, she drove us both back to her quiet street and little red brick house squeezed between two neighbors. Inside, last week's cleaning fluids and today's tuna still wafted on the efficient hum of air-conditioning. The home was dim and flimsy, the doors light in my hand, but Mickey told me this was how American houses were built, papery and hollow sounding when you knocked on the walls. I met Belinda, the illegal tenant who lived in the basement; Gonzalez, the incontinent cat; Poncho, the blind German shepherd; and Bill, Livia's companion, a black Cuban refugee who smiled and shook my hand firmly as he introduced himself. I smiled graciously at him and didn't let my eyes betray my surprise. I had become used to associating Mickey with a world that was different and peculiar.

We all took aluminum chairs out of the garage and crowded them together on the tiny six-foot-square landing outside Livia's front door overlooking the street, so we could enjoy the last hour or two of the salt-air afternoon before dinner.

Later that evening, we relaxed in the living room on a sixties-style sofa. Livia sat on her orange La-Z-Boy recliner, not really reclining so as not to mess up her careful hair, and talked quietly with Mickey about classical music and international affairs. Bill cut articles out of the *New York Times* and interrupted with points he emphasized by stabbing his large pair of scissors into the air. The only time anyone raised their voices or got even a little excited was when Gonzalez, the cat, made a loud shushing noise from behind the sofa, like an unashamed old lady in the next-door lavatory stall.

In the days that followed, Mickey took me on screeching graffiti-smeared subways to walk the streets of Manhattan. We went to the nude section of Jones Beach with Mickey's college friends, who took off their clothes, chatting casually among flapping breasts and penises, while I sat straight-backed with pretend savoir faire in my old-fashioned Zimbabwean bikini.

He took me to a baseball game, which didn't seem like a sports event at all. Yankee Stadium, with its big screens and cotton candy, its organ-grinder-style music, and fans singing along was more what I imagined Broadway to be; the players looked funny, even cartoonish, in their knickerbockers and caps. It couldn't have been more different from the splintery bleachers and thick-necked no-frills war rage of Rhodesian rugby or the leisurely weekend-long thwack and starkness of cricket on the lawn at the club.

At the end of August, Mickey was the best man at a wedding in Central Park. The bride, Erica Andrews, was a tall and beautiful California girl with a deep laugh, broad tan shoulders, and confident swinging blond hair. "Fuckin' shit" popped out of her mouth like languid hiccups as she swilled warm beer and lounged on the steps of her brownstone. Mickey told me admiringly that she mooned the bums on Broadway when they whistled at her, shocking them silent. New York feminism howled at me like a tornado.

Erica didn't seem interested in talking about her wedding dress, or the menu, or the flowers. She had no idea what her bridesmaids were going to wear. "What will your new name be?" I asked her politely, grabbing at the only possible detail left to discuss.

"Andrews," she said, frowning at my naïveté. I'd never heard of that, a married woman unflinchingly holding on to her own name.

"Mrs. Andrews?" I asked uncertainly. She stared at me curiously.

"Ms.," she said.

At the wedding the father of the groom showed up on a bicycle with a Walkman, and people in the congregation brazenly interrupted the ceremony to dance or disgorge drug-induced verbal rivers of good wishes.

Then Mickey took me to the airport and we hugged each other tightly, both wondering if this really was goodbye.

Gail had been frantic, calling Gillian daily, certain I was involved in all manner of depravity. Both of them were livid when, after six weeks, I finally returned to South Africa. Even Sharon and Lauren sounded tentative on the phone, as if they weren't sure they knew me anymore. Yet, invigorated by the pale shoots of germinating opinions, I felt bizarrely elated. I found work selling computer software and drove around Johannesburg with more confidence. I subscribed to *Time* magazine, which I tossed around insouciantly, bringing up casual political insights with my new boss.

Mickey went back to Philadelphia to finish his MBA and found a cold room in Powelton Village, a slummy and radical area near the University of Pennsylvania, where accommodation was cheap. We wrote each other. He called me often. His telephone bill crept higher than his rent.

After he graduated, he flew back to Johannesburg and asked me to move to America. I didn't really think about it. Still riding high on the exhilaration from our trip of the previous year, I remembered the admiration that would flicker across people's faces when I told them I had been to New York.

Manhattan.

It beckoned in neon lights with whispers of myth and fantasy. *If I can make it there, I'll make it anywhere:* step-kick, step-kick, and smile at the audience.

WHEN I ARRIVED BACK IN NEW YORK AFTER SPENDING THE SUM-mer with Mickey in South America, we weren't rushed to see the sights as we had been the year before. I returned casual and confident, an old New Yorker arriving home, playing to invisible Zimbabwean spectators sitting rapt and forward in their seats as they watched me jog along the Brooklyn prom-enade, sip cappuccino in Greenwich Village, and brave Man-hattan muggers on the alphabet trains.

Mickey and I rented a place in Brooklyn Heights and I em-braced the role of the woman of the house, anxious really for a familiar thread or rhythm, suddenly not as brave as when I arrived. Cowed by the choice in the supermarkets and para-noid about spending precious foreign currency (a holdover sentiment from the war), I bought tuna. We ate tuna casse-role, tuna salad, tuna sandwiches, tuna noodle-doodle, and tuna whatever-recipe-was-on-the-can.

Sometimes Erica called and invited us over for a barbecue at the brownstone where she and her husband, Martin, lived on West 98th Street. "Will you pick up a few packs of Nathan's All Beef Skinless Franks on the way?" she asked casually.

"What?" I replied, alarmed, frowning and ready with a pencil.

She repeated Nathan's All Beef Skinless Franks, four or five times, slower and slower, like a hand-cranked gramophone run-

ning out of spin. Venturing tentatively out of the tuna aisle, I
discovered the freezer section. There were dozens of bright la-
bels: pork, kosher, skinless, beef, foot-long, Oscar Mayer, lite,
chicken. I hunted through slippery cold plastic for the particular words Erica had given me, anxious not to disappoint.

When we got to Erica and Martin's brownstone, Erica
opened her door wide and greeted us with, "Fuckin'-shit-
it's-hot." She spoke loudly above the hum of fans, securing
damp strands of her hair with strategic bobby pins. Their
kitchen and bathroom were all one room divided by a shower
curtain, and once we had finished assembling dinner we
climbed onto the toilet seat, balancing wobbling trays of
hamburgers, and clambered out of their tiny bathroom window to reach a landing on a small deck with struggling basil
and tomato plants. We sat together on the deck (or was it part
of the roof?), knees almost touching around a dinner-plate-
sized barbecue, the sky above us far too light for stars. When
Mickey and I left to take the subway back to Brooklyn, I
breathed in the surreal quality of the New York air and wondered how to describe this new strangeness in a letter home.

In Zimbabwe, there are no real seasons. In June, it is a little
cooler; in October, hot. In January, hopefully, it rains. Planting
and reaping govern the pace of life in the rural areas, while
the pace of urban life doesn't change.

In New York, weather brings distinct collective changes
of mood. The leisurely unhurriedness of summer, the sharp
enthusiasm of fall, the marking time of winter, and the deep
lung-cleansing breaths of spring are not something you'll find

in the Michelin Guide, next to statistics about the Statue of Liberty. They are changes that pop up and surprise you when you are living there.

By the time the leaves started to turn and the air grew cooler, we had sublet the basement floor of a brownstone on West 94th Street from two women friends of Mickey's who were temporarily traveling in India. Mickey had found a job with a big commodities trading company in Midtown and was excited about his new career. I sometimes walked him to the 96th Street subway station. We walked brusquely, not really talking, both paying attention to his carefully planned route that guaranteed we would never have to wait at a red light. After a quick goodbye, I wandered slowly back to the apartment alone, less attentive now that I had nothing to be late for.

I wondered about the American women who were away in India. During those long days I tentatively touched their possessions, curious to discover what it meant in Manhattan to be female. One of them had a contraption that hung you upside down, your feet strapped into big buckled boots, and I stared and wondered at it—not sure if I should try or what it was supposed to do.

I flicked idly through their books, looking for more clues, but panicked when a tumble of naked photographs slid out of one of them. I guiltily stuffed the photos back between the pages, quickly wedging the book onto the shelf, simultaneously shamefaced at my prying and alarmed at tangible evidence of strong American women who knew how to be uninhibited and bold. I had an urge to seep into the shadows of that dim sublet apartment, my temporary sanctuary.

When my trunk finally arrived from South Africa, I unpacked it eagerly, but all my pastel-colored carefully coordinated polyester outfits seemed wrong in Manhattan. I stared at my permed hair and my plucked-thin eyebrows in the bathroom mirror, getting closer and closer until my breath fogged my image. "Even my face looks different here," I complained later, to which Mickey replied, propping up on one elbow, that most of the women he knew and admired at college didn't pluck their eyebrows.

Erica became my model for American womanhood. I wanted to be as nonchalant, confident, witty, smart, and sexy as she was. Although I couldn't bring myself to curse comfortably or moon anyone, I started to wear what Erica wore: a black T-shirt with jeans or tatty khaki shorts. Erica was disdainful of permanent waves and frosted hair, so I let my perm and my highlights grow out. Then I was disdainful of them too.

One cold Friday in February, when it was muted and snowy in Manhattan, Mickey and I went to Toronto for the weekend. I only had a few days of my visa left, and we thought we'd stay with one of his friends up there and grab another six months' stamp in my passport on the way back. But the American immigration official in Canada, squinting through his bifocals, pursed his lips, shook his head, and said no. I could use up the last few days on my visa only if I produced a dated air ticket back to Johannesburg or I could go directly back to Johannesburg from Canada now, circumventing the United States altogether.

Mickey and I had talked about marriage once before, so I

wasn't totally unprepared when he proposed in the Toronto Airport before our flight back to JFK, just out of earshot of the bad-tempered immigration official. I knew I loved him, but I didn't bother to picture what forever would look like in America, because I knew it was inevitable that life would quickly change. For the next few weeks or months or even years, though, I wanted to be near Mickey—to have his confidence and certainty about the world spill over and splash onto me.

We talked about a quick ceremony in the registry office, which seemed efficient and possibly even romantic in its own way, but Livia begged us to make it more of an occasion. So I looked up BRIDAL in the Yellow Pages, not really sure where to begin to find a wedding gown in Manhattan, and then picked a store that advertised "best selection" and "reasonable prices."

Through big warehouse doors I found floors of small stores stuffed with white tulle, lace, and billowing plastic bags, all watched over by people who looked stern and irritated. I tentatively wandered into one store where the salesman didn't look too gruff and declared that I was getting married. He asked me what I wanted, and when I said I didn't really know, he impatiently waved me toward the jam-packed racks. I pulled out a dress, any dress, there were too many of them for me to love or even see, and tried it on. I wondered, tilting my head at my voluminous bridal reflection, whether it was too much for a small wedding. I desperately wished I had a friend to ask—someone Zimbabwean, whom I could understand. It made no sense to ask Mickey to come back another day and help me choose.

The salesman came to look over my shoulder at my reflection in the long mirror. "Aaahh, beautiful," he said, clapping his hands together and smiling for the first time. "Now you can have that one long or short, in ivory or in white. The sleeves can be full, sleek—or sleeveless is also a possibility. The neckline comes in round, square, or V-necked. Do you think you'll want a train? A veil?" I couldn't wait to get the dress off. My mind emptied itself, revolting against the terrifying avalanche of choice.

I went to Bloomingdale's instead, found a plain cream dress in one of the fancier departments, and bought it. Although I didn't like it too much, I thought it would do, and besides, where else would I turn?

We had dinner with Mickey's father, Walter, a brusque business executive who could be briefly engaging but mostly gave you the impression that he had more important things to do. His new wife, Lore, clearly intimate with what was chic, suggested the wedding be at the Tavern on the Green in Central Park, and I snapped up her suggestion quickly, grateful I didn't have to think about it further. I wasn't sure what a string quartet was, but Jackie, Mickey's sister, generously offered to organize one. Mickey's close family and his Middlebury friends all came.

No one from my past or my family was there. To be fair, I wasn't sure I really wanted them. Sometimes, I felt like I interacted with Mickey's relatives and his friends like a deaf person pretending to understand sign language. The thought of my family—or friends, for that matter—squinting eyes at them critically, and then at me, before saying, "What on earth are you doing? Who *are* these people?" filled me with dread.

I wanted to be brave, defiant, even dismissively certain. And I wasn't sure I could do it with someone who really knew me watching.

On the morning of my wedding, I walked to a florist's on Columbus Avenue and bought peach-colored roses and some baby's breath, along with a few narrow strands of silky ivory ribbon. I carried it all home and then sat on the floor of our apartment, pricking my fingers on thorns and thin sharp wire, forcing the flowers into a bouquet and a spray for my hair. When Erica and Martin arrived (matron of honor and best man), Erica said my bouquet was *creative*. People used that word a lot in America, washed down with a splash of admiration: *Creative*—sigh—*aaahh*. In Zimbabwe, the closest translation of *creative* is *making a plan*. *Making a plan* is slightly different from *creative*, though. *Creative* means thinking up an alternative, in spite of all the choices. *Making a plan* means thinking up an alternative when you *have* no choice— like having to fix a bicycle with a hairpin because spare parts aren't available.

I wasn't being creative on my wedding day, I was making a plan. Although part of me wanted to be as casual and non-chalant about my wedding as Erica had been, here I was, fussing with flowers, making my fingers bleed. Another part of me, the Rhodesian part, would have preferred to be relaxing in a robe, having a manicure, sipping a glass of champagne, with Sharon, Lauren, Gail, Paddy, and Auntie Barbara all around, pampering me. I wanted the doorbell to ring and everyone to rush excitedly as I opened a big mysterious box

Mickey and me.

containing a magnificent trailing bridal bouquet and smaller posies for the bridesmaids, all carefully sprinkled with water and wrapped in tissue. There would also be buttonholes for the groom, one for the best man, and one for the father of the bride, if she had one.

9

In the beginning, marriage offered me a small identity and a direction, so puttering proudly in my new role as wife, I went looking for an apartment that Mickey and I could buy. I hadn't seen many apartments in Manhattan. Mickey's father had a penthouse guarded by an army of doormen who bent close-headed over *Victoria's Secret* catalogs. Erica's brownstone seemed far friendlier, with bohemian comings and goings of the people who lived on the different floors, and the fact that the bathtub was in the kitchen and their double bed next to the dining room table. It was fun to tell people in Zimbabwe that I was in a city where everything was upside down and I could laugh at it all. No, embrace it. I told the Manhattan realtor that I wanted a place with "character."

Completely bewildered after a few short weeks, and no longer certain I could cope with Manhattan character in quite the same way Erica did, I gratefully seized upon an ordinary yet large apartment off Amsterdam Avenue in the seventies. It was its size, really, that drew me. That and the generous porcelain tub with the black plug on a chain and the squiggly rust stains from the slow-running faucets, which reminded me of Zimbabwe (one of the British legacies in Zimbabwe are deep porcelain tubs). I also liked that it was on the ground floor—I couldn't imagine living in a place you could only reach by elevator—the thick burglar bars on the windows made me think of home, and there were no inquisitive doormen lurking to get in your way.

Mickey was less certain. "It could be noisy," he said, looking out of the bedroom window at honking cabs and feet hurrying past. Already, I was getting a nagging sense that Mickey was not the kind of manly man I was used to. Although his sensitivity had attracted me at first, it began to bother me after we were married. He didn't like cigarette smoke or loud noises. He complained about sitting in drafts. He got irritated if Sharon or Lauren called, forgetting time zones, at 2 A.M.

"I need space," I insisted, thinking of all my future Zimbabwean guests. "I want to be on the ground. I don't want to have to pass a bunch of noisy doormen every time I walk in," I told him definitively. It had become clear to me that opinions were what made you a person in America, so I snatched at them as they floated into my head and held on tightly, trying to clarify myself, to carve a place.

It was the lawyer we hired to process the property transfer papers who warned us not to go through with it. It was so clearly a bad buy that he took the time after work one day to look at the place, and to confirm that we—really, I—were out of our minds.

My experiment with confidence drained as quickly as bathwater out of that porcelain tub. I was reminded that opinions could be dangerous and decided it really was safer not to have any at all. Mickey chose a one-bedroom on the fifteenth floor of a prewar building on Riverside Drive that had a view of the Hudson if you leaned far enough out of the living room window. The halls had an airless old-sneakers smell. I had to take the elevator any time I left or came home, and a bevy of efficient doormen monitored our movements, held our parcels and dry cleaning, and kept homeless people out of the lobby.

I bought a soft cranberry-colored sofa, put it under the window, sat on it, and stared out onto the street below. Once the police roared in from both sides, sirens and megaphones blaring, after a tiny sprinting black man threw a gun into the bushes of the apartment building opposite.

But mostly there was not much to see.

Mickey worked at his desk. When he traveled I watched TV. Sometimes he looked up on quiet weekends and suggested that I read something, and I shook my head, feeling distant.

I know it sounds silly, but New York was so *quiet* after Zimbabwe. America was a place where life played out gently, only in the middle octaves. Sometimes I went walking and exploring. Mickey said I should always seem *purposeful* and not look people in the eye, so when I occasionally missed my street I kept marching on purposefully to the next block, before turning around and marching purposefully back, anxious not to appear lost or confused. Once a woman said, "Excuse me," and, worried, I quickened my pace, but then I felt bad and turned around to look at her, and she said apologetically, "I was just wondering if you have the time?"

On Thursday mornings, the New York Philharmonic practiced in Avery Fisher Hall, and they allowed listeners in for free. Feeling sophisticated, I went, then quickly wrote home to tell everyone about it.

But mostly I just stayed in the apartment. When Mickey and I went out together, I felt unfathomably resentful that it was usually me who said, "But it's still early" or "Let's have one more beer," wanting to find a way to tap into the old roar of rowdy parties in the sun, but compared to Zimbabwean men, Mickey barely drank.

We did go to parties and dinners in New York, quite often really. Most people I met, confident men and women with educations and opinions, heard my accent and asked me questions like "Do you have fraternities in England?" They always looked a little vague when they heard I was from Zimbabwe, one of the old colonial countries in Africa that used to be called what-was-it-again? Wasn't it brushed with something like white supremacy? Or was it?

"Oh, I know someone who went to Zimbabwe when it was still the Belgian Congo," one woman said confidently, although mostly I heard: "Is Zimbabwe part of South Africa?"

"No," I answered, deftly slipping out of the pigeonhole, enjoying a nanosecond of power.

"Where did you go to college?" would invariably be the next question, an attempt to bounce into familiar territory with a one-word reply that could potentially offer up a jackpot of information. Mortified, I would admit, yet again, that I had never gone to college, and for a moment they would look shocked, as though I had made the faux pas of drifting into the wrong social class, and then they looked embarrassed, having no idea of what else there could possibly be left to say.

On one occasion, at a party celebrating a young woman in Mickey's MBA class who had just landed a new job, the guest of honor asked me, "And what do *you* do?" Knowing I couldn't make *nothing* sound as exciting as *Wall Street at seventy thousand a year*, I blurted, "I'm waiting for a green card."

"What *will* you do?" she persisted.

"Temporary secretary," I said meekly. "But that's because I want to be able to travel with Mickey," I added quickly, trying to redeem myself.

"So you'll be content to spend the rest of your life just following Mickey around the world?" She said the words slowly, pronouncing them carefully.

"Well," I replied, trying to think fast, but she didn't give me a chance.

"I think that's very refreshing," she interjected, nodding straight-faced at her MBA girlfriends, who had all been listening.

. . .

IT WAS THE MID-EIGHTIES IN MANHATTAN. EVERYONE WAS HORRI-
fied that the Japanese had bought Rockefeller Center.
Michael Milken had made hundreds of millions of dollars in
junk bonds. The space shuttle Challenger exploded minutes
after launching, raining debris out of the sky that we all
watched on TV, over and over again.

Sometimes we went up to visit Livia and Bill in Yonkers.
Livia would fuss and feed us, keeping her house dark and
quiet so we could nap. Or we would have Friday night Shab-
bat dinners with his grandmother, Ruth, who lived in a tiny
apartment on Dykeman Street in the Bronx with a grimy
stairwell she ascended on the Sabbath. Ruth would pray and
remember in soft murmurs, rocking oblivious and out of time
to the sirens and ghetto blasters on her street.

Walter and Lore's friends were quite different from Livia
or Ruth. We ate with them in fancy Madison Avenue restaurants, sipped cocktails in their penthouse, and went to barbe-
cues next to the pool at their place in Larchmont. One of
their friends with coral fingernails and a clean white smile insisted that I not decorate our new apartment with anything
that matched because that was so "middle American."

If only she knew that I was trying to figure out what
"American" was so I could be just that. I wanted to be warmly
embraced by a tribe and community, as I was before—more
in Rhodesia than Zimbabwe—but I couldn't figure out how.
American flags were enormous and everywhere, the national

anthem as it echoed across vast baseball stadiums was stirring, but that was all there seemed to be. Underneath was just a confusing free flow of different people saying different things, everyone interrupting, trying to speak more loudly than anyone else.

Sharon came to visit me from Harare that first fall Mickey and I were married. She had been promoted to manager of a string of luggage shops in Harare and was dating Butch quite openly then, although they fought continually. Butch played water polo for the Zimbabwean national team and stayed out drinking on all-night benders, serious parties, after his games. Part of the reason for Sharon's trip was a sort of trial separation from Butch, but when she walked into my apartment there were four letters waiting from him.

It was such a relief to see Sharon—this flesh-and-blood appearance, my lodestar, my anchor, forever my reference point for what is true—her presence in New York somehow confirmed that not only Manhattan but I too really existed. I hugged her tightly. She put down her bags and looked hungrily at the cozy breakfast I'd prepared. "What's this?" she asked, picking up a round piece of bread with a hole in the middle.

"A bagel," I told her.

"Weird," she replied.

Sharon and I explored New York together, gossiping. While we admired the view from the Empire State Building she reported that Lauren was dating a very dubious man. Brett had long hair. He had Indian friends, went to parties with that funny foreign diplomat crowd, and was the only white person Sharon had ever met who even went to restaurants barefoot. Perhaps his odd behavior had something to do with him being a geologist?

It was hard not to wonder about Brett. Ambling through Central Park, we found a bench on the edge of the Great Lawn. "And you wouldn't believe Brett's parents," Sharon told me, widening her eyes for emphasis. Apparently, when Lauren visited their small farm in Nyanga, she discovered their house to be a chaotic jumble of floor-to-ceiling books. Brett's father wore little glasses and a long gray beard down to his waist. Lauren didn't even meet Brett's mother, Sharon giggled, until much later that afternoon when Lauren was exploring the property and someone scared the daylights out of her by yelling down from the high branches of a tree. "His mother's an ornithologist or something," Sharon told me.

"What exactly is that anyway?" I asked with a frown.

Mickey, Sharon, and I all went up to Maine, to see the real America on my first road trip out of the city. Everyone in New York admitted that Manhattan wasn't representative of the country, yet I found the city manageable in a way because I knew it was supposed to be strange. I was looking forward to visiting a small American town with ordinary folk trying to carve out their own ordinary path like I was, so I could be reassured.

It was late fall when we left on a wide gray highway that had three lanes going in either direction. When we got closer to Kennebunkport, Mickey sighed and said, "Isn't this pretty?"

mostly to himself. I knew Sharon saw what I saw: thick roads, lots of big green signs, and a whole stack of oddly shaped trees with brittle, dry leaves falling off them jammed tightly together like an afterthought on each side. I knew the word *pretty* must have scratched on her ears as an odd one for a man to use. But he was my husband now and I was an American—whatever that was—alongside him.

"Yes, look at how pretty it is," I said firmly. I even said *pretty* like Mickey did: "*Prurr-dy*. It's real *prurr-dy*." Sharon shrank a little, looking uncertain and left out. She didn't seem impressed, like I was hoping she'd be.

We stayed at what Mickey called an *inn*. It was a brown wooden building that overlooked a harbor where squat painted boats bobbed like toys. A friendly woman with tight platinum curls talked to us continuously, deftly maneuvering her enormous green-panted bottom in and out of tight spots, as she bent and twirled in search of registration books and keys. She showed us two musty-smelling rooms with stiff over-shampooed wall-to-wall carpeting and windows that looked out onto the harbor with blue gathered frills above those plastic shades I hadn't yet learned how to open without tugging them out of the window completely. "Er," I interrupted her as she was leaving us, "I was wondering if we can get some tea?" Sharon and I were both thinking of a nice pot with some cake. Maybe a warm fire. She paused and thought. "You should be able to get tea about two blocks down on the right."

It was difficult to hold hot tea in paper cups and sip it through plastic lids. They'd made it too strong. We had to ask specifically for milk. There was nowhere to sit down with it, so we walked down the street in the brisk fall breeze, the little paper flag on the tea bag beating against the side of the cup, flapping us in the face whenever we tried to take a sip. Mickey suggested we walk down Main Street and we did, admiring quaint buildings painted in lilac, pale yellow, and pink with wooden signs hanging from posts on little chains and streetlights designed to look like old-fashioned gas lamps. We peered into store windows and smiled at the clever things to buy. And then we crossed the street and stepped out of the olde worlde movie set and back into the regular world of gas stations and 7-Elevens. "Ah," Mickey said, striding down the block toward the brown shingle-sided inn, taking deep breaths, his hands pushed deep into his jacket pockets. "Isn't this great?"

Later we went out for lobster, because that was the special thing to do in Maine. Sharon and I were not expecting an elegant restaurant, but we did imagine there would at least be proper plates, linens, and cutlery. Mickey ushered us into a place that was crowded with diners wearing plastic bibs with pictures of red smiling lobsters on them. The tablecloths were made of paper. The waitress said, "Hi, guys," plonking down a basket with disposable napkins, plastic utensils, and little packaged butters. "What can I get you?" she asked cheerfully, wiping her hands on her apron, putting her foot on the bottom rung of my chair.

It's hard to pinpoint exactly what felt so disconcerting. Perhaps it was the waitress's overly familiar tone. Maybe it was the lack of self-consciousness with which the other diners wore their bibs. Maybe it was just that this "real America" felt so insubstantial, so shifting and capricious—so frightening, as though there were nothing really there at all.

Our food arrived with a paper boat of butter-drenched corn, and Mickey showed us how to eat the lobster—first breaking off the tail (being careful not to splatter the green stuff) and then prodding into the legs and claws with the little sharp fork. We bought a couple of beers and drank them out of the bottle, which we held clumsily with our buttery fingers. Both Sharon and I started to relax a little.

It was Sharon who noticed blueberry pie on the menu for dessert. We'd both heard about blueberry pie, but neither of us had tried it before, so we ordered a piece to share. Sharon squeezed her eyes closed, laughing, after the first bite. "Taste this," she said, pushing the plate toward me. I took a mouthful, and a startling shooting sweetness made me gasp. Giggling, we flagged down the waitress and asked her for some cream; "Sure thing, honey," she said, tripping off to the kitchen.

We were engrossed in conversation when the waitress returned, clumsily leaning over Sharon's shoulder with an aerosol can, which she aimed at the pie, noisily hissing out a quick high curl of fluffy cream. Then she stood back, smiling with the colorful can as if she were advertising a fly spray. "Enough?" she asked.

Neither Sharon nor I had ever seen aerosol food. Looking at each other, we began to laugh. We laughed and laughed, egging each other on—our shoulders shuddering, tears running down our cheeks—while Mickey and the waitress watched us, frowning and confused.

. . .

BY WINTER MY GREEN CARD CAME THROUGH AND I SIGNED UP
for temporary secretarial work. A note of disappointment
would consistently ring when I told an employment agency
that I hadn't been to college, after which they would pause a
little before filing my credentials in a different box, showing
me with a pencil point the wage scale for noncollege gradu-
ates. They liked my accent, though, calling it British no matter
how often I said it was Zimbabwean. Jobs they found me
largely involved answering the phone for companies who
thought I sounded sophisticated. Noticing my lack of college
credentials, employers slowly went over important information, like Tokyo being the capital of Japan and how to find the
ladies' room.

I worked temporarily at a publishing house, where they
taught me not to use the word *whilst* in business letters and
gave me permission to use *but* at the beginning of a sentence.

I shyly turned down a lucrative position at *Screw* magazine.

I eventually accepted a permanent job in an advertising
agency on Madison Avenue, where my boss sat under an
enormous painting of a dollar bill and next to a holograph of
his wife that blew kisses when you walked past. Reluctant
to check mail and halfhearted about returning calls, my boss
gave the impression of having arrived at this particular junc-
ture of his life inadvertently. Mostly, he liked to take off his
tie and slouch on the sofa with people from the Creative
Department, chatting, hooting, and thinking up clever lines.
Every afternoon at four, no matter what emergency might be

pending, he ran out of the office, yelling unabashedly, "Tell them I've gone to the shrink!"

Close to Christmas, he asked me to help him with the company sex competition. Every year, all employees voted on who in the agency they would most like to sleep with, he chuckled, and I was to type out this year's ballots, distribute them, and make sure they were all returned. "Do you think we should add a gay or kinky sex category?" my boss asked. I frowned, not knowing. "Maybe next year," he declared, satisfied.

I collected secret ballots; the agency was abuzz with whispers and intrigue. At the annual holiday lunch in a neighborhood Mexican restaurant, while I shyly struggled to appreciate the difference between a fajita and a burrito, with one hand vaguely wondering if the margarita I was gulping was alcoholic, and with the other fumbling a joint I'd been given and didn't know what to do with, someone stood up and announced, "The ballots are all in! The moment you've all been waiting for! The winner of the sex competition is—Wendy Kann!"

Laughter and flapping hands pushed me to stand. "Speech, speech!" everyone yelled. What was the proper response? Slap someone five? Act flattered? Indignant? The table where I was sitting was on a smaller, slightly raised section of the restaurant, so when I stood, I could see everyone very clearly. Jim, Mike, Sam, and Bob from the mailroom all whistled and waved at me. I recognized smiling faces from the media department, all the people from the bullpen, the research people, account executives, secretaries, copywriters, lawyers, all clapping hard and whooping. I looked down quickly at the table and muttered "Thank you," remembering what my boss had whispered when he first told me about the sex competition. "It's usually the real loose girls who win this thing," he'd said.

My boss would never have embarrassed me intentionally. He often gave me extra leave, sometimes even twice a year, so I could go back to Zimbabwe. Actually, everyone at the agency was incredibly nice, my friends at work once even planned a surprise farewell party for me before one of those many trips home. They scurried around all day with whispers, sidelong looks, and shopping bags of snacks, and then at five they all went looking for me. The food was artfully arranged in the boardroom. Balloons were rustling in a soft bunch from the ceiling. People were gathering, holding their plastic cups of wine or soda, asking each other, "Where is she? Where is she?"

I had escaped from the building hours before, ducking away from work and my life in Manhattan without so much as a backward glance, anxious to arrange the little presents I'd collected for everyone back in Harare. I was so single-mindedly focused on escaping America that I usually began blissfully sinking into my old Zimbabwean life days before my plane actually left. I hadn't even thought to say goodbye.

NOW, WHEN I WENT BACK TO HARARE, I LOOKED OUT OF PLACE with my crumpled black cotton T-shirts, unplucked eyebrows, and straight hair. Everyone there said, "You're *so* thin," and it wasn't a compliment. Gail happily told her friends on the phone, "My daughter's home from New York." Gentle and intimate, she whispered that I'd forgotten to put lotion on my legs or that a brighter pink on my lips would be nice. "How about a little red?" she would say lovingly, pulling up the ends of my plain brown hair and letting it fall again. My mind twirled, feeling sophisticated and childlike, close and distant, happy and sad all at the same time.

I went down to the Harare Sports Club bar with Sharon and Butch, and someone asked me what my new name was. I tossed my head, like Erica had done when I first met her, and said "Black" in a nonchalant tone. A row of puzzled men on bar stools stared back at me, knees wide, thick hairy thighs tightly stretching short shorts. Someone offered, as if I were a bit slow-witted and hadn't really understood the question, that Black was my name when I was single. I countered, trying hard to maintain conviction in my voice, "I see no reason why women should give up their names and identities when they choose to get married"—which bought another thirty seconds of frozen blank attention before they all turned around, shaking their heads slightly, and went back to their beers.

Mickey sometimes came back to Zimbabwe with me. He would quietly fish the ice out of his drinks with a fork and hesitate before boldly peeing arch-backed on the lawn after dinner. I preferred to go home alone. Mickey was a Jew, his mother lived with a black man, and for my few precious weeks in Harare I just wanted to rest there unthinkingly, without disappointing anyone.

Sharon and Butch, although still not married, had bought a little brick house with turquoise gutters and a secondhand electric security gate in a suburb called Alexandra Park, which was close to the center of Harare, in the middle of things, where they both liked to be. They had a dark blue pool, bright

roses, orange red-hot pokers, lilac agapanthus, and an old avocado tree with weary limbs that the pendulous green fruit
pulled almost to the ground. I was most comfortable there,
drinking tea or wine on the veranda with Sharon and Lauren.

Lauren had moved to Karoi, the small town in northwest-
ern Zimbabwe where my mother had spent her teenage
years, to be with Brett, who was working there on a mining
project. She found a job keeping the accounts for a local gas
station, and they lived a quiet, happy life in a cottage on a
nearby farm for two years. But everyone at the Harare Sports
Club agreed that Brett was rather strange, so one day Lauren
had an impulsive public affair with a beer-drinking rugby
player who dropped her after a week.

"It was a terrible mistake," Lauren cried later on the phone,
but it was too late: Brett wouldn't take her back. So she
drifted in Harare, trying several different jobs and dating different men. She went to England, to maybe work or travel,
but called me after a couple of months. "It's freezing here,"
she complained, so I sent her money for a coat, but still she
found London foreign and confusing and hurried home just a
few weeks later.

On one of my trips to Zimbabwe, after Lauren had been
home from England a year or so, the three of us went with
Butch and some of his mates on a trip to the Zambezi. You
need to get up early to fish on the Zambezi. There are those
moments in the damp dawn when the crystal air still teeters
in a cool and hesitant way, before the day grows confident
and rolls out boldly, flattening the entire valley in a stifling
blanket of heat. Sharon and I crawled out of our tents and lay

tummy-down on an already warm rock, breathing in the fish-mud smell of the river while Butch and his mates set themselves up on the bank. Half asleep, we listened to the whir and plop of their lines. A fish eagle swooped and screeched, like a soul with a haunted past. Anxious doves tickled back and forth on nearby branches, calling *hoo, hoo*, soothing it.

By nine, it was already getting hot, but still no one spoke, imagining we could cling to coolness by not breaking the spell.

"What's Lol *doing?*" Sharon suddenly whispered to me. I looked up, and there was Lauren, beautiful and slim in her new swimsuit, wading knee deep in the green waters of the crocodile-infested Zambezi, pulling, obliviously, on everyone's fishing line.

"I think she's showing off her new suit," I said, squinting into the rising sun.

"Trying to impress Jan, maybe," Sharon said, looking at the puzzled face on Butch's young single friend.

"Lauren!" Butch bellowed. Lauren looked at him innocently. "You're tangling up all the bloody lines!" And Lauren looked down at the web of tackle around her legs and then at the irritated faces on the bank and, suddenly realizing what she was doing, looked to the sky and laughed helplessly, and soon Sharon and I did the same. Mickey always said it was the most amazing sound when we really and truly laughed, the three of us together.

I'M NOT SURE WHY COLUMBIA UNIVERSITY'S SCHOOL OF GENERAL Studies in Manhattan accepted me. According to British standards, I was without the necessary qualifications. Perhaps the fact that I was from Zimbabwe intrigued them. Perhaps they thought that at twenty-seven I could contribute all sorts of interesting perspectives.

Little did they realize I was so lost I had no perspective at all, not knowing whether I was an American, a Zimbabwean, or a Rhodesian, and so overwhelmed by other women and their lives in New York that I was even bewildered about what it meant to be female.

I sat eagerly in the front row of my lectures, pencil poised, considering my entire degree as something of a test, or race. I took electives on classical architecture and Renaissance art, read Walt Whitman and Henry David Thoreau. I bought thick textbooks on astronomy, geology, and French and took seminars in history and colonial literature, the only colonial there, not contributing a word. I sat through discussions on gender and race, hungry for guidance, quietly taking down notes.

As in the years immediately after my father died, it reassured me to imagine that although I might appear shy and tentative, I was really strong and resolute, as he had been. After all, I had proved this when, like him, I had unflinchingly cut my mother out of my life. A small part of me was even proud that I hadn't weakened when Sharon and Lauren begged me to visit her deathbed.

Now, I stoically decided to slice off my Rhodesian history too; it had clearly taught me nothing of value. As I walked home though Riverside Park every afternoon, holding my jacket tight against the bitter wind off the Hudson as fat city pigeons rose and swirled in gritty clouds, I constructed a new, more acceptable American self out of my lectures; breathing in brisk air, I let my relieved mind build in slow logical layers as I counted up my A's like Scrooge.

When I saw how Americans learned, their sensibilities slipped more into focus. In the beginning, I was shocked at the way other students loudly and unself-consciously released any unfinished musing that happened to float into their heads, like noisily belching in public. I didn't really interact too much with my peers, although one morning I did notice the one girl who usually sat next to me in my Nineteenth-century Art History class looked awfully miserable, so I asked her what was wrong. "I broke up with my boyfriend," she mumbled.

"I'm so sorry," I said.

"Although there is one good thing about fighting." She smiled sadly.

"What's that?"

"The fucking afterward."

I graduated Phi Beta Kappa and magna cum laude, though it wasn't as if I had slid into a warm bath of learning and leaped out yelling *Eureka!* What I did receive was a direction and something to hold on to, to steady myself, as well as a way to communicate with and understand Americans that I didn't have before, even if Columbia didn't make me bold. I still longed to let uninhibited words tumble easily from my mouth, or careless expressions cross my face, but I wasn't there yet. Mostly, I continued to live my life tentatively from the outside of my body looking in, instead of solidly from inside of myself looking out.

A few months after my last exam at Columbia, I was called down to Federal Reserve Plaza to interview for my American passport. The woman going through my papers announced, "Your husband ain't American."

"What's that?" The woman in the next-door cubicle leaned over the partition.

"Look. It says here he was born in Japan," my woman told her. It was true. Mickey's father was working in Japan when Mickey was born.

"That don't matter," said the woman next door.

"He's got to have naturalization papers," my woman insisted. "He don't have 'em."

"He's got an American passport. He votes," I offered, but no one paid any attention and I was sent briskly on my way with a mountain of forms to fill out and a long list of certificates to track down. Less than a month later, before I'd even begun, notification arrived for me to attend a swearing-in ceremony at the court, which I did, promising my allegiance to the flag, and I became, in rather an abrupt and seemingly arbitrary way, an American citizen. About a year after that, Sebastian, my darling son was born. An American and now a mother too.

IT WAS A RELIEF TO SINK INTO MOTHERHOOD—TO FINALLY HAVE a noble reason to be. I had read that children were comforted by their mother's heartbeat, so I carried Sebastian close to me all day. If he so much as whimpered during the night, I gasped with the pang of abandonment and rushed to gather him up.

That Christmas, Lauren came to New York. Having established something of an identity for myself, I felt I was now in a position to guide her. I loved having her with me in Manhattan—laughing hard when she forgot that the temperatures inside and outdoors were quite different, grinning proudly as she gaped at perfectly triangular Christmas trees (conifers in Zimbabwe struggle, gasping with dryness and heat). I danced deftly through New York dinner parties now, chatting about literature and politics, but watched, with an empathetic pang, Lauren's pasted-on smile hiding a quietly desperate face.

I wanted her to move to America and live close to me. Mickey arranged a date with an eligible young investment banker, though it was I who insisted that she go.

"But what will I say to him?" she asked unhappily.

"Oh, I don't know," I said. "Whatever you want," pushing her out the door, looking at her beautiful clear skin, her concerned hazel eyes, certain she wouldn't have to say anything at all.

I got up before five the next morning, when Sebastian woke, and peered into the living room where Lauren slept on the pull-out sofa. She wasn't there. Did she spend the night with him? Had something happened to her? Why hadn't she called? Weeping softly, I handed Sebastian to Mickey and ran downstairs.

She was curled up in an armchair in the lobby, her light brown hair falling in mermaid swirls against the pale blue.

"Shhh," the doorman said when he saw me. He had draped his thick gray coat over her, keeping her warm. "She lost her key and didn't want to wake you."

"Of course she could wake me," I said tightly, although knowing it wasn't his fault.

"Lol." I shook her gently, trying hard to compose myself. "Come upstairs. Did you have a good time?" I asked.

"It was terrible."

"Then why are you so late?"

"I met another guy on the subway."

"The subway?"

"His name was Lewis Love."

"Lewis *Love*?"

"He invited me to his apartment."

"You went?" I said, wanting to sob again.

"Just for coffee," she said sleepily, crawling onto my sofa and closing her eyes.

I tried to push her to study, to read, to tether herself with knowledge, as I had done, but she had no patience for it. She hated her course on off-Broadway theater. "I can't do this," she declared, stabbing at her comparative religion notes with her pen, blinking at me in frustration, flicking away her hair. "What do I care about the Bhagavad Gita?" she added irritably. "I don't even like Trivial Pursuit."

"But I'm not so sure about Choma," I told her, as she slit open letters from Richard, a handsome Zambian tobacco farmer she had recently met in Zimbabwe, who wrote almost daily.

"Well, I know I could never live *here*," she replied.

I stared at my little sister, lying on my lonely New York sofa, then bent to draw a soft blanket to her neck. The membrane between us had grown suddenly thin and permeable again, and I was washed with profound, inexplicable sadness.

Lauren left Manhattan with a shudder. Just over a year later, I sent her fifteen yards of ivory-colored satin and tulle for a wedding gown and went back to Harare for the ceremony. It was jacaranda season, and the entire city was floating in pale purple blossoms, baking hot.

In a mysterious way, Lauren's marriage made New York feel cold and empty again. When Mickey came home from work one evening and tentatively said he'd been offered a position in Hong Kong, I didn't have to think about it. I couldn't wait to leave.

10

Mickey, Sebastian, and I moved to Discovery Bay, a new development in Hong Kong on Lantau Island that attracted foreigners with young families. Disco Bay, as we called it, was a place where broad swaths of buff-colored, same-style apartments and houses were strung down the mountain like something hurriedly rolled out of a Shenzhen assembly line. When looking for an apartment on Hong Kong island itself, I had been shocked to discover that children there were expected to play in parking lots, and mothers to push strollers across busy highways in order to visit a park or a beach. Disco Bay was something like a suburb of Hong Kong; it had playgrounds and green space. Cars were forbidden completely, and people there got around by bus or bike or, if you were lucky, golf cart. Filipina amahs, or maids, took care of housework and children.

There were one or two clubs with tennis courts, which were too hot to use for most of the day, and murky swimming pools, which seethed with club members on baking summer weekends.

By far, the biggest houses in Discovery Bay were on Seabee Lane, but they frequently languished empty, the developer's extravagant mistake. Expats, generally only in Asia for two or three years, and even local Chinese, were reluctant to take on a home where the three-story living room required scaffolding to change the lightbulb, but to me, a big house felt comforting. Unlike the apartment Mickey and I had almost bought on Amsterdam Avenue, there seemed to be no particular fault with these places, so we signed the lease. Having moved in, I inhaled the familiar air of entitlement with relieved and thirsty gulps.

The air in Hong Kong was wet. It curled around linens and shoes, fattening them with moisture, feeding them with lacy gray patterns of mold. It lingered with unhurried mustiness on your tongue. It trapped odors of sweet-fetid durian fruit and stinky dried fish piled high in rickety stalls. It buoyed the sound of clattering trams and jackhammers. It held the heavy smog tightly in its muggy haze, coloring it fuchsia over the harbor in the evening light.

Us *gweilos*, or foreign devils, stuck together, and I made friends quickly. *Are the vegetables in the market sanitary? Do they really eat dog and snake? Do Chinese workmen always leave cigarette butts in your toilet?* We drank lattes in Disco Bay Plaza, sat around on beach benches in the heat of the late afternoon, and on Christmas or Thanksgiving we all got together, like family.

Hong Kong was a weaning, in a way. It was a first-world city with a slowly thinning drip of colonialism, a neutral environment that lapped against my ideas of good and bad, home and not-home just as I lapped against Mickey and he against me and we softened each other, blurring the edges that made us different, shading us into something more of the same.

I started painting. Our three-story living room echoed so badly I bought huge canvases, easily copied modern art from photographs I found in decorating magazines, and then hung them on my expansive walls to try to muffle the sound. I taught my new friends in Disco Bay how to make cheap oil paintings for their temporary living rooms too, and we all sat in my vast, empty entrance hall, gossiping, dabbing paint, pausing only when Anita, my amah, interrupted us midmorning with an enormous tray of tea. And then, even after every wall of my yawning house was covered and the place stopped echoing, I continued to take the half-hour ferry across to Hong Kong Island to buy shopping bags full of turpentine and oil paint from the one art supply store in Causeway Bay, addicted to the soothing focus of brush on canvas, casually giving away my stacked artwork when it began to clutter. "I won't be offended if you don't want it," I was always careful to mention.

After a year in Hong Kong, my daughter Claudia was born high on Victoria Peak in Matilda Hospital, where it's a degree or two cooler and verdant with languorous ferns and cycads, banana palms and bamboo. Nurses there brought tea with milk and sugar, midmorning and midafternoon. Big fans on high ceilings chopped unhurriedly at the dense, humid air. The staff even babysat your newborn if you wanted to leave the hospital for champagne and a romantic dinner with your husband.

For the longest time, British colonials forbade the Chinese to live up on the Peak. Although those rules had long changed, the Matilda still catered mostly to expats. Chinese hospitals were concrete cubes of activity, where staff doctors or nurses seeing to hundreds of people generally had no patience for personal preferences or time to spend on gentle explanations about your care.

With two small children, I was determined to become the perfect mother. I initiated ambitious arts and crafts projects with my toddler; I energetically read to my six-month-old; my shelves began to sag with books on parenting and child development, and I was proud that other women started to approach me with their toilet training problems or when their toddler suddenly started to bite.

Disco Bay was a relatively small development in a corner of Lantau, the biggest of the many islands at the mouth of the Pearl River that make up Hong Kong. Sometimes, on the amah's day off, we rented a junk with a few other families and took the kids to explore different smaller islands, or other villages on Lantau, which were only accessible by boat. Even in much of winter the South China Sea was balmy, the breeze of movement lulling. The giant Buddha, built high on the green mountains in the middle of Lantau, caught the sun and glimmered, just visible from our boat. Huge cormorants swooped, mewing plaintively, or tottered on dark rocks as they held out their dripping wings to dry while our engine *chug-chug-chugged* past on the way to somewhere new for lunch.

Usually, you could smell the rustic island or village before you docked there. The odors of fish, trash, and chicken excrement emanated outward toward us on little beats of damp air. Sinewy tobacco-brown fishermen puffed on smelly cigarettes and picked over their garbage-entangled nets, while we teetered between tubs of grouper and abalone, frogs, and mussels on the dock. You heard mah jong tiles rattling aggressively and glimpsed black-clad women playing within their shadowy dwellings; mahogany ducks hung in tiny storefront windows from large silver hooks. We'd eat a dubious lunch of fish-off-the-dock and duck-off-the-hook, all slapped down on a table by a brusque cook in his undershirt, served in a restaurant with a dirty floor and old food caked in the crevices of the chairs. The *real* Hong Kong, more seasoned expats would boast; see it while you can.

We all knew that in 1997 the colony would be returned to the People's Republic of China, so that in 1993, when we arrived, an anxious sense of running out of time was already pervasive. Local Chinese nervously lined up for hard-to-come-by residency permits at the Canadian or Australian embassies; longtime British officials resigned themselves to returning to a place that no longer felt like home. Most *gweilos*, however, wouldn't be there for long, and it was they who delicately sipped the last days of Empire, looking forward to the handover as an excuse for yet another party.

And party they did. Still longing to be blissfully spontaneous, I carefully watched the Disco Bay "yummy mummies" who attended Wednesday Ladies' Nights in Wanchai and Lan Kwai Fong. I sat rapt on playground benches on Thursday afternoons while they regaled me with last night's adventures at Carnegie's, which had a wide bar counter you could dance on, or China Jump, which had a dentist's chair that could be tilted back in order to pour alcohol straight down your throat. I heard the last ferry back to Disco Bay at 3:30 A.M. was packed and hilarious, unless you missed the boarding ramp completely and fell into the filthy harbor, in which case Chinese ferry personnel barked in irritated Cantonese while impatiently fishing you out.

The "yummy mummies" also had plenty of parties in Discovery Bay itself. One notorious event on Headland Drive (by day, the most tasteful area, in contrast to my galumphing house on Seabee Lane) started like any other, they said. We stood giggling, supervising our kids down the curly slide at the beach, dishing out juice boxes, while the mummies enthralled me: It was a humid night, they said. Dozens of people stood mingling politely on that Headland Drive lawn, murmuring near flickering candles in a multitude of languages. They dipped crudités and crunched chips, drank beer out of bottles slippery with condensation, and quietly sipped wine out of plastic disposable cups. Then, unexpectedly, a German woman draped a languorous arm around the Scot next to her and began to slowly lick his startled nape before sprinkling salt on his already sweaty skin. Popping a lemon wedge in his gaping mouth, she lazily licked the salt on his neck, downed a shot of tequila, and then casually retrieved the lemon from his mouth with her teeth (taking the time to include a bit of a smooch). The Scot blinked quickly in an anxious way but did not look unhappy.

Someone turned the music up and body shots caught on fast. Brits licked Finns, Belgians sprinkled salt on Poles, and Australians stuck their tongues far down French throats. The night felt hotter and the music curled deep in that pulsing teeth-rattling way. Laughter rang high from a rowdy little knot in one corner of the garden, where a woman was wiggling her hips in subtle figure eights, singing, *if you think I'm sexy . . .* as she ran her palms over an Italian bodybuilder's chest, slowly unbuttoning his shirt, a case of Reddi Wip (I knew all about Reddi Wip now) left over from her waffle stand at the elementary school's International Food Festival at her feet.

Still singing, she pushed the bodybuilder flat onto an adjacent picnic table, smoothing him out like a tablecloth. Unbuttoning his pants, she turned his waistband down just a tad before ejecting four wobbly trails of Reddi Wip from his chin, down his neck, and ending with his groin. She balanced four brimful shot glasses on the stretched-flat place between his hipbones while others gathered around, grinning, with lipstick smeared and eyes glazed. The Hong Kong night bore down.

They told me it was not difficult to find women eager to lick the cream off the Italian, grab a glass at his groin with their teeth, and throw back their heads to swallow the shot in one gulp. Then things got still crazier. An angry Frenchwoman shouldered her way through to her grinning husband, who was blissfully flat on the picnic table, and slapped him across the face. People grabbed their own cans of Reddi Wip and offered up their sweaty bodies to be sprayed and licked. Men with white-smeared faces dipped squealing, tipsy women into garbage cans filled with ice (the beer was long gone). The stereo blew a fuse, and a too-drunk Belgian (perhaps too shy or too late with the cream) hopped up and down, trying to get his short, chubby bottom over the wall to plug the stereo into the neighbors' outlet, not noticing that by this point no one needed music. A slinky British woman left with a handsome Hollander (they were both married to other people); the prim choir mistress from the elementary school had drifted off with the bodybuilder. The stragglers staggering out as the sun rose over Hong Kong Harbor and ran loose-legged piggyback races down Headland Drive, past the unimpressed Chinese security guards and buses full of people on their way to work.

KNOWING WE PROBABLY WOULDN'T BE IN HONG KONG FOREVER, Mickey and I decided to send Sharon and Lauren a ticket to visit us after four years there. Then, suddenly feeling guilty that I also had a grown-up half sister now, I invited Shiobhan to join them too.

Vonnie, twenty-five, came tripping off the ferry in a very short miniskirt with men buzzing all around trying to take her bags. Sharon (now married) and Lauren, both pregnant, struggled out much later, grumbling and dragging Hanna, Sharon's two-year-old, as well as their combined heavy suitcases.

We four sisters had lots of giggly fun in Hong Kong. We went back and forth on the ferry to Central District on Hong Kong Island; Vonnie was intent on stocking up her wardrobe and Sharon wanted a string of pearls and conducted furtive negotiations to secure a fake Louis Vuitton bag. Lauren, I noticed, had a new aura of wisdom, or perhaps it was just resolve, about her. Having earned a little spending money at the hot grain depot in Choma counting sacks of corn thrown on and off trucks, she now spent it frugally on little items for her farmhouse—a stainless steel teapot, a few colorful prints for her living room walls.

It had taken Lauren almost five years to begin thinking of Choma as her home. In the beginning, there was the initial shock of her isolation, then early frustrations with selling *kapenta* fish and breeding chickens; when squatters moved onto their farm, a year or so after she married Richard, she was finally at her most despondent.

Panicked, she wrote or called often during that time, explaining how she had been taking her usual evening walk to the dam when she noticed a whole village of thin ghostly people who had seemingly arrived from nowhere, their naked babies crying, their worn possessions in bags and sacks, rusty bicycles dropped like heavy black skeletons in the long grass on Lauren's property. "They were building huts!" she told me. "They were chopping down *my* trees!" she said, suddenly possessive about a farm she'd nearly grown to despise. Angrily, she questioned the intruders and they replied, clearly embarrassed and possibly a little frightened, that Lauren and Richard's struggling tobacco farm was their ancestral land.

This was probably true, just as the air and water had also belonged to their ancestors before the white man arrived in Africa with confusing ideas about race and ownership. Now, much more than a hundred years later, title deeds were firmly knotted with power, economics, and greed; passions had been inflamed by history and hunger.

Terrified that her and Richard's meager assets would disappear altogether, Lauren first tried to use the law to disentangle the problem. For a year she drove long hours up to Lusaka, the Zambian capital—and sat on plastic chairs in bare waiting rooms with lazy fans stirring the smell of other people's sweat—to consult with lawyers and government officials. But the law is often just a guideline in Africa. The mechanics of the continent often work more closely with an unseen and equally unpredictable system of threats and promises, webs of moral obligation inside which it is hard to find beginnings and endings or know where to look for a solution.

In the meantime, the squatters plowed, planted, and irrigated with her precious dam water, nodding and saying "Good morning" to her when, her furious expressions shaded by a broad straw hat, she took her marches with the dogs across the farm.

In desperation she turned to a traditional African healer, who told her that if two hyenas were to appear on Semahwa, the squatters would see them as witches, interpret their presence as a bad omen, and leave of their own accord. But catching two hyenas, transporting them to the farm, and making sure they stayed within farm boundaries seemed like a tall order. Besides, there was also the possibility that Richard's laborers would see the hyenas as witches and leave too.

Lauren eventually called me, weeping with frustration. "I've had enough of Zambia," she said. "Richard has agreed to find a farm manager's job in Zimbabwe. I can't wait to go home."

Since her marriage, Lauren had always looked for excuses to recharge herself at Sharon's little house in Harare, and once they decided to move back to Zimbabwe, Lauren seemed to find those excuses more often. Butch, the wild aspects of his character now more muted (he was content with Friday nights at the Harare Sports Club Bar), had an electrical contracting business; Sharon had left her chain of luggage stores and was publishing calendars and diaries. She had also discovered a passion for singing, becoming so proficient that people begged her to sing at weddings and funerals, which she did over the weekends.

Lauren, having signed paperwork allowing her to take her few pieces of furniture out of Zimbabwe when she married Richard, now had to get permission from the relevant Zimbabwean authorities if she wanted to come back. She began to buzz Sharon's security gate in Alexandra Park more and more often, weary-eyed after hours in her little Mazda, with forms, passports, and birth certificates all bulging in her purse. More distracted than usual, she once ran over Sharon's cat and often lost Sharon's house keys. Still, Sharon fussed over her. She put roses in Lauren's room and bought South African wine and imported olives from the OK Bazaars, and they sat on the veranda in the evenings, celebrating.

Lauren went to the passport office on Herbert Chitepo Avenue and stood in long queues, filed papers, then stood in long queues again. "We're very sorry," the black man behind the counter always said, shaking his head and smiling sympathetically at her.

In desperation she arranged meetings with prominent white men that my family or friends knew. "I'll take care of it," they would reassure her importantly, but when she came back, weeks later, they returned her brown envelopes of papers and forms with perplexed, even bashful expressions. "I'm sorry," they would say. "There seems to be nothing I can do."

"Please," Lauren begged, returning to the first man at the official passport office. "But you are British," he told her kindly.

"You can take it," Lauren told him, rummaging in her bag, pushing her British passport under the glass that separated them. "I am a Zimbabwean," she said. The people behind her grew impatient and stirred a little—they had been waiting a long time too. "Please," Lauren said again.

"I'm sorry, madam." The man sighed, pushing her passport back to her. "You should have given this up after Independence."

"But I didn't know," Lauren pleaded. The passport official shook his head and then glanced beyond her, nodding at the next person in line. Disbelieving, Lauren stood immobile for a few moments longer. Then someone with damp chocolaty skin edged passed her, beginning new noisy business in Shona, as if she wasn't there.

She returned to Zambia despondent. For months after that,

she helplessly watched those shadowy squatters plant their rustling corn, slowing consuming Semahwa, leaving Richard and her in limbo, belonging nowhere. England, although a possibility, was a foreign and austere place. Besides, what on earth would Richard do?

And then there was a local election in Zambia—not usually a big deal. Someone or other won or lost, and within a short while the police arrived unexpectedly on the farm, truncheons swinging, guns in holsters. When they got close to the ragged village, the squatters started to run. Barefoot mothers scooped up wailing children; police ignited huts and corn; the little village burst into flame.

Lauren and Richard had their land back. A strange combination of fear and guilt remained lodged in their throats, but those are not unusual emotions in Africa, and after a week or two the feelings started to dissipate. Impassioned by the promise of a new direction, Richard redoubled his energies on the farm. Invigorated by regaining something she thought she had lost, Lauren made a concerted effort to settle in Choma and began to invite the other district women over for tea. Richard laid a water line so she could plant a lawn and roses. They decided to have a baby.

Wandering around Hong Kong now, Sharon, Lauren, and I had all reached a level of certainty and contentment in our lives. Having lived so long away from Harare, I was grateful to finally get to know Vonnie, who made us all roar with her intelligent, witty sense of humor. The four of us went to the Peak and to see the "real" Hong Kong on rustic islands, but since Sharon,

Lauren, and I were all pregnant (I with Samantha) and tired easily, Vonnie was sometimes left to explore on her own while we sat around on my sofa and had Anita bring us tea.

Lauren confided she was still lonely but determined to make a go of Zambia, and Sharon hugged her while I put my hand on her knee; glancing quickly at each other over her head, we assured her she would be fine. Clearly shaken by their experience with the squatters, Lauren often bought the conversation back to them. "You wouldn't believe how brutal the police were," she told us, frowning at the memory. "They attacked the women . . . they beat the men . . . there were babies and children . . . ," she murmured. "And then," she said, "about a month later, Richard and I noticed one of the elders from the squatter village in Choma. We tried to leave quickly, but he saw us, and while we stood there clumsily, wondering what to do, he simply raised his hat and said 'Good morning' as if nothing had passed between us at all."

THE LAST MAJOR OUTPOST OF THE BRITISH EMPIRE, HONG Kong was officially handed back to the Chinese on June 30, 1997. Prince Charles came out for the ceremony, as he had for Zimbabwe's almost two decades before. Twenty tons of fireworks were to be detonated from eight barges in the Hong Kong harbor at midnight, and visitors were expected to arrive by the thousands. Local Chinese were encouraged to bring their radios into the streets so they could sing along to "Canto Pop" in a city-wide celebratory karaoke party. But then it rained. No, it didn't just rain—the heavens opened and let loose the torrential, drenching sheets of a tropical downpour.

We watched the festivities from the Jardine Matheson building, an old British landmark. Just over a century before, William Jardine and James Matheson had, in the face of massive Chinese resistance, imported vast quantities of opium into China, initiating what became known as the Opium War, a three-year military conflict that China lost, leaving Hong Kong to be grabbed by England as a prize. Jardine House, slap bang in the middle of Central District right next to the Star Ferry, promised a great view of the ceremonies, thanks to the many big round windows, like a ship's portholes, that gave the building its local name, House of a Thousand Arseholes.

It was raining much too hard to see anything out of those famous windows, so we settled down with our champagne and confetti and watched it all on TV. Soldiers in kilts and tam-o'-shanters paraded in the downpour. The pipes and drums of the Black Watch presided, as they had fifty years before in India, wailing a steady marching tune. Prince Charles stood in his white navy uniform at an outdoor podium next to the harbor, intoning in a proper royal voice, "In a few moments, the United Kingdom's responsibilities will pass to the People's Republic of China," as rain poured off the edges of his low-peaked cap in seamless silver veils. A Scotland Yard man darted up with a royal umbrella, but Charles waved him off. "There have been times of sacrifice suffering and courage," Charles went on, unflinching.

"He looks a bit wet," a British woman watching on TV

commented, as thundering rivers of water pushed the prince's broad epaulettes askew, jangling the heavy medals on his chest. After a short while, no one was concentrating on his words, mesmerized as we were by his unflinching royal stoicism. His hands never left the podium and his words never faltered, as water streaked over his eyes and trickled into the corners of his mouth. When he finished, the band struck up "Rule Britannia" and TV cameras panned the soaking locals, huddled with radios under plastic sheeting and cheap Chinese umbrellas. Prince Charles snapped a quarter turn as the blue Hong Kong flag with the small Union Jack in one corner was lowered for the last time. Then he, the Hong Kong governor (whose manly tears were evident even in the rain), and Lavender (the governor's wife, whose skirt whipped viciously around her pale legs) all waved with proper British aplomb before hunching against powerful winds to board the royal yacht *Britannia*, sailing off solemnly into the South China Sea.

Before dawn the following day, four thousand troops and twenty-one armored personnel carriers from the People's Republic of China quietly crossed the border into the former colony. Photographs of them there, bristling with guns, stared out at us from the *South China Morning Post* when Mickey and I stumbled out of bed for coffee. I think everyone felt surprised and more than a little unnerved to suddenly see Chinese troops in our friendly Hong Kong papers.

I recalled the night after the first elections in Zimbabwe, how incongruous it had been to suddenly have Robert Mugabe, the archenemy, confidently address the nation on our cozy Rhodesian Broadcasting Corporation TVs. I was left then, as I was now, with a sense of uneasiness—a nagging reminder that laws, police, media, army, and government had been usurped by threatening strangers and the safe, predictable order to the world had abruptly vanished into delicate, bewildering uncertainty.

On the surface, not much had changed in Zimbabwe immediately after its independence—as little changed in Hong Kong. Police officers removed royal emblems from their caps. New officials promised tolerance. Different coins appeared without the profile of the queen.

In Discovery Bay, I still painted and sat on playground benches in the late afternoon. Not particularly perturbed by the handover, other expats there nevertheless spoke with resignation about one day having to settle down and go home. Children need aunts and uncles my friends all agreed. It's time for grandparents and responsibility, they said, a little wistfully, remembering it had been fun. By then, Mickey wanted to go home too, and I knew it was best for my children to grow up American, firmly settled in a place that had a better chance of forever staying the same. I was sorry to leave Hong Kong, but I had become quite cavalier about loss by then and pretended to shrug it off.

11

The first selectwoman of Westport, Connecticut, once boasted to the *New York Times* that hers was a Norman Rockwell town. Remembering the confusion of Manhattan, I wanted to live in a tidy American suburb where I would be happy, I thought, in a spacious house with a pool and a beautiful yard. So in the late summer of 1998 we bought a white clapboard colonial with neat black-green shutters on a serene Westport lane. Towering trees arched and rustled, throwing leafy spans of light. The air smelled of pine and had the salty-mud taste of Long Island Sound.

At first I was a little intimidated by our suburban American house. Fat groundhogs waddled through my yard; raccoons overturned the garbage. There was an attic, and something large in there whirred. The basement was filled with an alarming assortment of pipes and tanks that clanged and coughed in an unpredictable way while I was down there doing the laundry. Mickey busily twirled dials and switches, making sure that the air inside was just right. Later in the year, he spent a lot of time popping out screens and popping in storm windows, climbing on ladders and scooping leaves out of gutters, and inspecting the hemlocks for mites. I didn't remember Zimbabwean houses—or even ones in Hong Kong, for that matter—being so complicated.

Although we hired gardeners to help, they only came every so often, and their services were expensive. The previous owners had planted a costly sapling awkwardly in the middle of the yard, and I inquired from my new gardener what it would cost to move it. He pursed his lips, walked to the place I'd hoped it could go, kicked the soil there, and ambled back to the sapling, trudged around it slowly, stamping the ground, testing its give. He plucked off a single leaf and turned it over and over in his hand, considering for a few moments. "Well, we're pretty busy now. Maybe we could schedule it for the spring. . . . Five hundred dollars," the man finally announced.

The last time I was in Harare, Sharon noticed a similarly obtrusive shrub right in the middle of *her* lawn. We were sitting on her veranda when she drew our attention to it.

"Do you think that tree blocks the view?" Sharon mused.

"Maybe," Lauren replied, squinting at it.

"It might look good near the irises," I confirmed.

"Thomas!" Sharon yelled. When Thomas appeared, she instructed, *"Ta ta lo one"*—jabbing her finger at the offending bush—"over there," and she pointed, indicating its new spot.

Thomas nodded—"Yes, madam"—and disappeared to get a spade.

OUR MIDDLE DAUGHTER STARTED PRESCHOOL AND, ALTHOUGH I hadn't asked, the director there assured me that Claudia would be physically and emotionally safe at all times. "That's wonderful," I replied. Sebastian, a second-grader by then, was enrolled in the local public school. I double-checked with Mickey. "Do school buses here come all the way to your house?"

"Uh-huh," he confirmed.

"And baseball is *really* called Little League?" I was shuffling through a mountain of medical forms, liability release papers, and extracurricular options, uneasy that I still had vast gaps in my knowledge (I only discovered that shoes needed to be polished when I was about thirty).

I joined New Neighbors. They had coffee mornings, book clubs, wine-tasting events, and excursions into New York. I signed up for the dinner club. Crown roast of pork was quite easy, one of my New Neighbors assured me, though I spent two days making sure the chops were neatly aligned, the stuffing flawlessly light, the white paper decorations (which I laboriously fluffed out with tweezers and a toothpick) not too greasy, and all perfectly balanced on those irregularly shaped bones.

I managed to make friends. PTA assignments were often

quite complicated, and yet they offered a way to get to know other mothers in the hours it took to build the Great Wall of China out of sugar cubes or spray-paint thirty pounds of macaroni gold. Sebastian's school looked straight out of the movies, with a big American flag in the parking lot, little American flags in the office and each classroom, and narrow gray lockers lining the halls. Cheerful red banners above each door had a cutout of an apple and a teacher's name written in friendly letters. Sebastian learned how to say the "Pledge of Allegiance." He went for play dates at other houses and happily announced, when offered meat loaf for the first time, "It's just like in *The Simpsons!*"

Carol, one of the mothers whom I met at school, was especially helpful in advising me on all the trinkets, candies, and cupcakes that were needed for the many class parties. After one such event, the teacher took the kids out to the field to run off the sugar before the afternoon bus, and Carol and I were tidying up.

"Would you guys like to get together this Saturday?" I asked, as we scraped most of the streamers and frosting I'd bought the day before into the garbage.

"Hmmmm, it's the Super Bowl weekend." She frowned. "We're taking my parents up to our condo in Stratton . . . my brother's meeting us . . . I've got a sister flying in . . . the kids . . . you know," she said, shrugging. "It's about time," she broke off to call to an older woman who was walking through the door. There was something thick and tangible between Carol and this woman—a kind of intimate knowing warmth that I imagined myself wrapped in.

"I brought you lunch," the woman announced.

"Thanks," Carol said, grabbing the bag. Then she called back to me as she hurried off, "Let's be sure to make it another time."

I discovered that age had done nothing to diminish the old ache that came with watching mothers and their daughters. In fact, that particular love seemed even more alluring now and, as I cheerfully waved to Carol, I felt myself briefly tumble into a familiar terrifying place, as if behind a glass, where the world was barren and bewildering.

I MISSED PAINTING, BUT WITH SAMANTHA LESS THAN A YEAR old, and without an amah, there was little time for oil paints and turpentine. Besides, although my Westport home was big, it wasn't as vast as our house in Hong Kong. After dropping the older children at school, I usually took Samantha down to the local coffee shop, where I ordered a cappuccino for me and a paper cup of milk fluff for her. I considered myself a good mother; it was the only identity I had, and I clung to it resolutely. Still, sitting there, I sometimes felt discouraged. There was the sheer shock of taking care of my own children twenty-four hours a day. Then there was the tangible competitiveness of parenting in Westport. Mothers here strained to become ever cleaner, safer, more patient, and more creative with birthday parties, camps, and educational opportunities. Laws made it a crime to leave your kids alone in the car, even if it was snowing and you had to run into the cleaners'. Ladies at the New Neighbors coffee mornings assured me this was a good thing because children get abducted in America. Besides, imagine if you were caught? You'd have social services at your door, and your name would be printed on the crime page of the Westport News, along with the names of those who stole potted plants from Izzo's Nursery and pocketed lipsticks from CVS.

Once I took my kids up to explore Devil's Den, an enormous nature preserve a few minutes to the north of us. It was beautiful up there in the fall, with lakes and snapping turtles and long twisting paths strewn with wood chips. It felt good to go to a place where my children were quickly red-cheeked, and I took the opportunity to use my new *Science for Your Kindergartner* to give them all sorts of lessons about moss and leaf decay.

Of course, though I tried to make it fun, no one was particularly interested in moss or leaf decay. The older two spotted a rocky outcrop and ran ahead. I stumbled behind with Samantha on my hip shouting "Slow down!" and "Don't climb that!"—which they did anyway. When I finally caught up with them I circled the base of the rocks, prowling and handicapped, pathetically calling out "Be careful," and "I think you should come down now," but then, relieved, I glimpsed a fellow mother up there with two of her own small children. I called out "Hi!" and waved to her. She peered at me warily. "I'm stuck," I shouted, pointing to Samantha. "Can you keep an eye on my other two?"

She hesitated, then shook her head. "No," she said, "I'm not at all comfortable with the liability aspect of that."

. . .

MICKEY'S MOTHER BEGAN TO DRIVE OUT FROM YONKERS ONCE A week to help with the children, and I took up photography—first catching the world in a neat frame, then enjoying peaceful nowhere time in the darkroom as slowly revealing images floated up. I joined an exercise class where we played air guitar to Bruce Springsteen, shimmying our shoulders to sultry songs about love. The instructor smiled and reminded us before we left, "Breathe in the healing power of the universe to illuminate the perfect light that exists just within you," and I sucked down great lungfuls of air, hoping she was right.

Katie, a new friend, invited me to her birthday party. When I opened her sparkling invitation, a cupful of shiny confetti fell out onto my kitchen floor. Wanting to show my enthusiasm, I called her and accepted immediately.

Perhaps fifty or sixty women arrived at Katie's house, giggly and excited, with pink and purple packages trailing colorful ribbons and bows. We drank champagne and they told sorority stories and summer camp adventures. Did you ever meet so-and-so at college? they asked one another. Do you remember the days when root beer floats cost a dime?

They included me too. "Where in England are you from?" They smiled. "Or is it Australia?"

"Zimbabwe."

"Oh."

I noticed a Chinese woman sitting quietly and went to talk to her. "Have you lived in Westport long?" I asked.

"Maybe two years," she replied.

"Where were you born?"

"Shanghai."

"How do you find . . . America?" I asked, hoping I didn't sound too desperate.

"Well, it's very different," she said, and we spoke at length about the differences. I told her I had lived in Hong Kong and, unasked for, gave her advice in my bossy older-sister way. We sat there, slouched on the sofa, peeling and popping edamame beans together, as I began to feel quite comforted and good about the evening. Maybe Wei and I could even get together sometime for lunch.

Katie came over. "Are you having fun, sweetie?" she asked, pursing pink lips, not waiting for an answer. She put her hands on my new friend's shoulders. "Girls, girls," she shouted above the noise. Someone turned the music down. The girls stopped dancing and looked at Katie with flushed, expectant faces. "Wei has been invited here tonight," Katie said, pausing for effect, "to give everyone a genuine Thai massage!"

When I got home later, Mickey had left the garage doors open for me, as he always does if I go out in the evening on my own, with careful little lights leading up the stairs. I quietly crawled into bed and cuddled up very close to him.

"How was it?" he asked sleepily.

"OK."

"Just OK?"

"Yeah." I could feel Mickey as if on waves, his breath rising and falling, rising and falling, tumbling him deeper into that soft place on the edge of sleep. I had never spoken to him about how shaky I felt our relationship was those early years in New York, although I'm sure he had felt it too. I snuggled a bit closer to him now. Married for fourteen years, of course we grumbled at each other occasionally, but mostly I marveled at how he had stayed so miraculously the same. Mickey still asked me questions and listened intently to what I thought, and I consistently liked how I saw myself reflected back in his eyes. It was a reassurance I had become used to reaching for, a goal I was inching toward.

"I love you," I whispered, hugging Mickey tighter.

"I love you too," he murmured.

SHARON CALLED ONE DAY TO ASK WHETHER I'D BE PREPARED TO accommodate Misti, her friend's twenty-year-old daughter, for a couple of months in exchange for help with the children. I leaped at the opportunity. Just before leaving Harare, Misti noticed her passport had expired, so, not thinking anything of it, she simply got out a pen and changed it. She arrived at JFK wearing canvas Bata shoes and speaking in a familiar comforting accent. Like I had once been, she was delighted with real yellow taxis and the Manhattan skyline. She marveled at the towering green trees of Connecticut, squealed with excitement at her first squirrel, and was incredulous that Westport lawns simply rolled trustingly one into the next, without the rude divisions of fences and gates. She picked up bagels off the dirty floor and offered them back to the children; she walked outside barefoot; she understood every word I said and also filled me in on the Zimbabwean gossip I'd missed—"Did you hear Sue Barnard got divorced?" or, "You must remember Sally Peterson's cousin"—bubbling on, linking me to my past, reminding me that I belonged to a clan and was a part of a warm human web after all.

I especially liked Misti's chatty stories about my sisters. "Mum says Sharon's so good with people—and *so* organized," Misti told me. "And she has such a gorgeous voice. Did you know she sang at Cathy Donvan's wedding?" I didn't. "And did you hear Sharon's trying for a third baby?" Misti enthused. That I had.

"And Lauren, darling little Lauren," Misti went on. She had relatives up in Zambia, so she was totally up-to-date on Lauren's activities too. "I hear Lauren has the most *beautiful* little boy. She really seems to have settled down in Choma now," Misti prompted. "I know they had those terrible squatter problems."

I regaled Misti with the story of Luke's birth, when Lauren, eight and a half months pregnant, had gone down to stay with Richard's mother in South Africa; most white women left Zambia to have their babies. Richard arrived, luckily, the day before Lauren went into labor, and called Sharon, who in turn called me in Hong Kong, and so began five hours of an urgent circle of conversation: me calling the little village hospital in KwaZulu Natal, me calling Sharon in Harare, Sharon calling the hospital, Sharon calling me in Hong Kong. Between us, I think we drove the two nurses in the Scottburgh clinic crazy, though Richard was ecstatic for any excuse to leave the delivery room and perfectly happy to give us minute-by-minute reports on Lauren's progress (although for a good half hour just before Luke crowned he was totally unavailable, having escaped to walk the dog).

Lauren's voice was weak and teary when I finally spoke to her. "He's so . . . amazing," she said. "I'm already nursing him. . . . I can't believe it, Wend," she said, a little tearfully.

When Misti left America, as I knew she must, I hugged her tightly, desperately sorry to see her go. "Be sure to phone when you get to Harare this Christmas," she said, and I told her I would, knowing I probably wouldn't. My time there with my sisters was so rare and precious, I didn't want to use it up on other people. I wanted to put my hand on Sharon's belly and feel the new baby kick. I wanted to hug my two nieces, Hanna and Niamh. I wanted to marvel at how Luke had grown and smile at his first words. I wanted to see Lauren, the lost baby sister I had carried into our old house in Mount Pleasant those many years ago, at last happy and strong.

I never did.

LUKE

Luke.

12

It was August 27, 1999, a bright morning in Zambia during those dangerously tilting days immediately after we buried Lauren. I held Luke tightly on my lap. Lucy lay on Lauren's black-and-white checkerboard kitchen floor, her head in a shaft of bright sun, her face raw and ravaged, oozing drops of perspiration and blood. She whimpered softly and sometimes cried out as Caroline, an ex-nurse from another farm, leaned over her, trying to remove her stitches.

Exhaling deeply, Caroline sat back on her heels. "Sharon, would you mind checking one more time whether there are any sharper nail scissors?" she asked.

"I've turned the place upside down," Sharon said. "There's nothing."

"How many more?" I asked.

"About seventy," Caroline said, bending over Lucy's face again, getting back to work.

Luke fussed a little, anxious in my arms, still not comfortable with me. I had only been on the farm six days, and the four leading up to Lauren's funeral I'd been so distracted by the swirl of people and the digging of her grave, that I'm not sure I even held him until the night we buried her. It was late and cold by then, and everyone had been drinking on the lawn in front of the farmhouse for hours when Sharon found me there in the dark and whispered urgently, "Richard's struggling."

I rushed into the dimly lit house where Richard, sitting on his bed, was staring at Lauren's lotions on her dressing table, while Luke thrashed, exhausted and hysterical, in his arms.

"I'll take him," I said, grabbing Luke and snatching up a thick blanket with my other hand as I hurried down the wide hall, kicking open the screen on the kitchen door, hoping the sudden cold air on Luke's face would shock him calm. I wrapped him tighter in the thick blanket and sat on the cement step close to the boiler fire, holding his limbs down so he couldn't flail them, rocking him hard, crying too.

Luke fell asleep almost instantly, and as he did I sat there in the dark listening to the popping fire and the murmuring voices from the other side of the house. I loosened the blanket from around Luke's face so he could breathe easier. His forehead was grazed from the accident and I touched the dried blood softly, then noticing he was starting to sweat a little at his hairline, I loosened the blankets some more. He was incredibly tall for his age really. I picked up his grubby foot and squinted closely at the cut on his ankle; it was quite deep, and I considered whether it should have had a stitch. Too late now. I dusted red dirt off his knees and shins before wrapping him up again and rocking him, more gently now, feeling a little neglectful that he wasn't in his pajamas and hadn't had a bath.

I had to leave Zambia a few days later. Lucy was far from recovered. Caroline had managed to remove all the stitches, but Lucy's face was very tender now, and raw. Her neck and shoulders were also painfully stiff. Still, knowing there was no one else for Luke, she had agreed to come in to work, and Richard had promised to pick her up from the compound every morning because she had difficulty walking that long road.

I worried whether he would remember. Richard was moving as though under water, responding to voices in a kind of lag time, turning to face you a moment too slowly, asking you to repeat the question. Neighbors promised to help, but the closest one lived an hour away. Even meager groceries were a forty-five-minute drive into Choma, and the only vehicle Richard had now, the one with torn seats and gaping holes in the floorboard, felt like it wasn't going to last.

When I got to Jan Smuts, the airport in Johannesburg, I called Mickey while waiting for my connection to New York. "How are the kids?" I shouted, above echoing announcements and whirring engines outside.

"Missing you," he said, hesitating a little before adding, "Claudia's been wetting her bed since you've been away. Seb's taken to stomping up the stairs and slamming the door at the slightest provocation, and Sam's been crying for her mommy every single night." He laughed a little. "We can't wait for you to get home," he said. I felt torn in two. "Listen," Mickey went on, "I've hired this girl, and she will still be available for a day or two after you get back. Should I keep her on?"

I closed my eyes trying to think clearly. "Well," I said, "what are her hours?"

"Hours?" he asked. "She's living with us."

WHEN I ARRIVED BACK IN WESTPORT, I CALLED ZAMBIA CONstantly, dialing and redialing endlessly, struggling to get through. I pestered Richard: Did Luke eat? Did he sleep? Did he cry? Sometimes I pestered Lucy: What time did you get to work? What time did you leave? Are you tired? If everyone was out, and one of the gardeners, Francis or Robson, ran in to answer the phone, I pestered them: How is the bwana? Did you plant carrots? Did anyone mend that washing line? Afterward I called Sharon, who had been calling everyone too (although she also included people from neighboring farms on her list), and we compared notes.

We decided to go back within three weeks. Richard and Lucy could hold on until then, we thought. We would stay in Zambia a month and paste over the hole that Lauren had left.

In the meantime, I busied myself buying Cheerios, Pampers, nontoxic paint, washable markers, Pottery Barn mugs, sharp nail scissors, Flintstones vitamins and Betty Crocker's brownie mix. I spoke to Westport psychologists to learn about children and grief, studied my vast library on child-rearing, and spent hours at Kinko's laminating notes on the subject. I knew Richard would never read a whole book.

In brief moments when I wasn't calling Zambia or Zimbabwe, or when I ran out of particular errands for Luke, I felt terrifyingly empty. It was as though my spirit, always so quick to flutter or burrow, could no longer find a way back into my body at all. In quiet hours, I tended to drift back on my years away from Africa, which now seemed wasted, fumbling and floating nowhere. Whenever I stopped to think, I was engulfed by an unbearable yearning to go home.

I tried hard to integrate myself. I saw a therapist in Westport and we explored the dry cracked bowl in my chest, unable to loosen it and so it stayed there, tight against my throat. I told her my dreams: carrying heavy burdens into dark underground places and fighting my way to Zambia through angry waters swirling at the lip of Victoria Falls. I described how that remote Zambian district had rallied for Lauren's funeral, banding together tightly with casseroles, extra mattresses, and bouquets. She cried, plucking at tissues meant for me.

I scanned the Yellow Pages for PSYCHICS AND MEDIUMS in New York City, mailed in a $250 postal order, and waited impatiently for a telephone appointment. I didn't know then exactly what I wanted to hear: Was Lauren impressed by all the flowers at her funeral? Did she have particular instructions for Luke? Did she laugh the night she was buried when Sharon, sobbing so hard, reached out to steady herself and accidentally put her hand on a chameleon?

When the medium finally called, she spoke in a ho-hum

and workaday way. "Once my mind is clear I'm a channel to all who dwell in the afterlife," she said brightly. "Anyone who knew you or your husband might come through."

Anyone?

"And you are *not* to interrupt me except with a quiet yes or no," she added as an afterthought. She sighed wide and deep and breathed noisily through a long pause.

"Do you know someone whose name begins with E?" she murmured, her voice suddenly dark and throaty.

E?

"I see someone smoking a pipe."

A pipe? My mind tripped into blind corners, trying to keep up with her.

"Hmmm, hmmm." She droned on, relentless. "I have an older man coming through. . . . Or it could be a woman." I listened carefully through the incantation in her words. "The name begins with F . . . or maybe J."

"Joan?" I said, alarmed. *My mother?* There was an irritated little pause.

"I said not to interrupt me," she snapped. "I was going to say *Joan*." Breath snagged in my throat. I could hear her muttering, recomposing herself.

"Joan says she is sorry," she said at last.

Blood roared deafeningly in my head. I felt I was slowly slipping underwater—my face was wet and I suddenly tasted tears

"Sorry," the woman repeated, thinking I hadn't heard.

I couldn't speak, and the silence waited there emptily. I squeezed my eyes tightly together, willing my mother away. I fought to stop myself from tipping into that bottomless well of sorrow and guilt, furious my mother was making me think of her.

The medium's breath plowed on, thick and heavy, and I trembled tightly, and the two of us lingered there, teetering in the afterlife.

"There's someone else," she finally panted, the air trapped between my teeth trickling out slowly. This had to be Lauren at last. I imagined her fighting her way through the mists to tell me something brief and important, a sisterly touching of the fingertips that would make everything all right. "I see a beautiful woman. . . ."

"Yes," I said.

"I see a foreign country. . . ."

"Yes, yes . . ."

"I see a car crash. . . ."

I felt a tightening in my stomach. I clung to her loud and labored sounds.

"I think I'm reaching Princess Diana . . ." the medium gasped, at last.

I DECIDED TO LEAVE MY OLDEST, SEBASTIAN, WHO HAD ONLY started third grade the previous week, at home with Mickey. I would take Claudia and Samantha with me. The tropical diseases specialist in Greenwich, Connecticut, raised his eyebrows when I told him I was taking a four-year-old and an eighteen-month-old to Zambia and adjusted his glasses, opened his desk drawer, and riffled in his files for a piece of paper, which he pushed across his desk toward me. It was the list of the shots he recommended: Hepatitis A and B, meningitis, tetanus-diphtheria, measles, typhoid, cholera, TB, yellow fever, and rabies. I smiled and inclined my head politely. I had really only wanted a prophylactic for malaria, something you can find at any pharmacy in Harare, right between the chewing gum and the Vermox for intestinal worms.

"Lariam is the most effective antimalarial," he said definitively, but warned, "It can cause psychotic episodes or hallucinations. If you notice anything strange you should stop taking it immediately. But most people who take Lariam only suffer vivid dreams and sleeplessness," he went on, attempting to reassure me.

"Oh," I said, wondering whether he had ever spent the night with jet-lagged children. Anxious that he should perceive me to be a responsible mother, I filled the prescription and Samantha, Claudia, and I took our tablets.

By the time we had flown from New York to Johannesburg and then from Johannesburg to Victoria Falls, in Zimbabwe, all the crayons and coloring books had been lost, there was Play-Doh on my seat, sour milk had soaked Samantha's last pair of pants, and my T-shirt was smeared with dozens of small handprints, caked remains of meals and tears from twenty-four hours before. We emerged from the aircraft blinking and disoriented, Samantha coughing a little from the smell of dust, Claudia clutching my hand tighter when she noticed the gyrating, wailing, leopard-skin-clad dancers with ostrich feathers in their hair beating their drums and performing on the tarmac for the tourists.

When Sharon's flight finally arrived, she stumbled out carrying her eighteen-month-old across her chest, pulling a heavy bag, and dragging her older daughter, Hanna, by the hand. Hanna had just turned four. Sharon's younger daughter was a towheaded imp with a funny Gaelic name, spelled *Niamh* but pronounced *Neeve*. Before we left the building, Samantha and Niamh were squabbling.

When Richard arrived he seemed pleased to see us. In the weeks since the funeral we'd all been simply holding on, but now we were together, it felt as though our anxious grief could move forward and ease. He had borrowed a canopy for the back of his pickup. "In, Hanna," Sharon instructed firmly.

"I don't wanna be in the back!" Hanna wailed, holding on to her mother's leg tightly.

"Well, there's no room in the front," Sharon said impatiently, picking her up and dumping her in. Hanna continued to wail. Sharon looked a little sheepish. She knew I read books about self-esteem and proper parenting and probably thought she was doing it wrong. She took a deep tolerant breath, forced a smile, and said, "Well, how about I get in the back with you for a little while?" At that Niamh cried, also wanting to be stuffed among the hot suitcases. Sharon muttered crossly, her momentary patience gone completely. "I'm not sure I can cope with all these bloody kids."

We stopped at the border, where Richard reminded Sharon to watch out for cheeky baboons, then at a gas station in

Livingstone to buy a few cold Cokes before starting our long baking drive to the farm. Finally, after an hour or two, Sharon beat furiously on the glass window of the truck's cab to say she couldn't take it a moment longer, and we rearranged ourselves, with me taking a turn on the thin cushions in the back.

It was dusk by the time we got to Semahwa. The flames in the outside boiler were stoked high and crackling, heating enough hot water in the tin drum above it for warm baths all around. Robson and Francis helped with the children and the luggage as we burst out of the cramped pickup, groaning and stretching, dropping sandals and sunglasses, forgotten Coke bottles from our laps clattering onto the gravel. For a moment, the watchman stepped away from his own little fire behind the water tower, wiped his hands on the seat of his faded, thin pants, chewed on nothing toothlessly, and regarded the excitement and goings-on through creased and crumpled eyes.

Lucy appeared with Luke clinging to her tightly. She held herself stiffly, wincing as Luke buried his face deeper into her neck. She smiled at me shyly, her caterpillar-like braids rearing around her head. Although her face had almost healed, her eyes were drained and exhausted. "Come on, mate," Richard said to Luke, in an overly cheerful voice, pulling at him. "Come and give your aunties a hug." I stood with Sharon and all the cousins expectantly. Luke whimpered. His long legs curled tighter around Lucy's slim body; his little fists only briefly releasing to clutch at bigger bunches of her blouse. "Luke, don't be silly," Richard said, in a slightly gruffer tone, pulling at him harder, until he managed to pluck him off, Luke's legs and arms flailing like a bug.

I had come so far it was hard to keep from grabbing hold of him. But Luke arched his back and wailed loudly, so after squeezing him tightly for a second or two, I put him down and let him run back to Lucy's skirts. It was getting darker. Samantha and Claudia watched me trustingly—their sanctuary in this bewildering new place—but I was barely aware of their presence. Slowly inhaling the smell of dust and sweat, I was slipping into an ordinary African evening, warm and gentle. The crackle of fire, shrill crickets, and distant contented cattle sounded like the beat of my heart.

13

Semahwa felt different. Late September now, the last rains had been in May, and colors were sucking into brittle, pale shades. The people who had been bustling about at Lauren's funeral had all gone home, leaving an eerie vacuum where sounds rang clear and sharp in infinite quiet. I was nervous there in the beginning, awake in the dark, sweating next to Samantha, both of us tossing inside a tangling mosquito net as I listened to faraway drums and the distant howl of dogs. The night was heavy and forever. The walls of Lauren's little house felt thin and frail against immeasurable blackness.

Perhaps it was the Lariam that made my dreams so startling, or the sudden snapped twig and jagged beam from the watchman's flashlight, cutting quick erratic lines across the worn curtains in my room, that made sleep so hard.

I wondered what the old man outside with his thick woolen hat was protecting us against, not yet understanding that the answer was nothing. I didn't know then that Richard paid him a few pennies a night, as he did the man who threw logs onto the flames to heat water for evening baths, or the two gardeners who took care of the dry patch of lawn near the house, mostly because they were there. The so-called security guard simply smoked marijuana and dozed all night next to his fire behind the water tower. Once, during a particularly dry season, dozens of cattle had broken out of their corral and trotted bellowing and lowing, right up to the house, noisily chewing up every speck of vegetation. Even that hadn't been enough to stir him.

I would know it was nearly daylight when I heard distant clanging on the still-dark air—the noise of a metal plow disk beaten with an iron pipe—the sound of an African farm starting its workday. Then, after a few minutes' pause, came the squeak of rubber-soled sandals on the cold red-polished cement floor as Richard strode down the long hall on his way to supervise the day's duties and delegate farm tasks. "Wait," I whispered loudly, disentangling myself from Samantha's limbs, struggling out of the gauze, patting the floor for my jeans, anxious not to wake Claudia in the other bed or Sharon and her children in the next room, running to catch up as Richard unlocked the kitchen door and pushed open the screen. Dogs flooded our legs and ankles, barking and yapping, their tails beating hard on our calves.

Even in the hottest months, southern Africa is cool in the early morning. The old pickup, damp with dew, spluttered into life on the third or fourth try, giving the little yippy Jack Russells time to leap through the windows into the cab and Chunky, the hefty Rottweiler, to heave himself up into the flatbed.

Richard nodded imperceptibly at Lauren's grave as we drove past. "I told her yesterday I was on my way to get her sisters," he said, glancing at me quickly. Sharon and I often included Lauren as if she was still part of our chatter, but Richard had never spoken that way before. "She would have been so happy to have you here," he went on, looking at that barren mound of sand and stones that caught the dim light under the still-black bark of the msasas. The flowers we had used to cover that heap had long since disintegrated and blown away. I turned my head, unable to find the words to reply.

As we arrived in the compound, the clanging on the plow disk was deafening. Half a dozen shirtless men yelled and hupped in unison as they pushed an old tractor down a small slope, cheering as it coughed into life, straining to hitch it to a trailer while other people noisily clambered on, all arguing and gossiping, shouting for latecomers as they pulled away, loud voices and cigarette tips slowly receding into nothing.

Seemingly deserted now, momentary silence settled over the compound, caught in the thinning darkness. But then the sun slowly erupted, powerful and red, cracking the gray horizon, glinting on broken windows. Old ladies emerged to sweep the dirt outside their homes while toothless husbands muttered to their reflections in cracked mirrors they had carried outside to shave. Barefoot children trickled out of huts, cadent and mellifluous, boys scampering, girls with heavy siblings on their backs, all lining up to fill buckets and old plastic bottles at the one faucet in the middle of the communal area. Richard and I circled back to the house with the Jack Russells running ahead of us, eager to claim the couch. Patrick, the houseboy, set tea on a tray with a stained cloth, a chipped sugar bowl, Lauren's Hong Kong teapot, and the new Pottery Barn teacups I had brought with me from America. We pushed the dogs off the couch and watched the BBC news on TV while we waited for Sharon and the children to wake up.

Of course, the biggest priority for Sharon and me on this trip was to set up an efficient and long-term child-care schedule for Luke. That first morning we cornered Lucy for her input on the subject, and she suggested that we employ her niece, Sandra. Since one of our concerns was to employ a person Lucy could work with, a niece sounded like a good idea. The village where Sandra lived was not far, Lucy assured us. She would send word, and Sandra could arrive on Semahwa in "very few days."

That being arranged, we looked for other ways in which to organize Richard's and Luke's lives. Sharon took on the kind of chores that involved long lists in her diary: how much the Super Store had paid Richard for his small crop of potatoes, a reminder to herself to send Richard an updated calendar from Zimbabwe to replace the one from 1994, a note for me to send Tupperware from the States. She shook old curtains out of the linen cupboard, laboriously hammered up frills and swags, bustled about in the farm office, staring accusingly at the untidy piles of farm accounting ledgers with her hands on her hips. She was certain that they needed her attention too.

I pursued Luke. I wanted to hold him close to me, to carry him around all day safely enfolded in a mantle of love. Familiar now with the components of healthy toddler development, I was determined he not be disadvantaged. My plan included working on his gross and fine motor skills, fostering his creativity, and building his self-esteem. My books had suggested water play, sand play, blocks, Play-doh, stories, singing, dress-up, crafts, and painting. I didn't have much time, and for gross motor development I needed at least a jungle gym and a couple of swings, so I decided to start with that.

Midmorning Richard came back to the house, and I cornered him. "I'm going to build a playground."

"A *playground*?" Richard sounded impressed.

"Yes. I'll need old tires, ropes, and gum poles. And labor," I added. "Do you have anything in the compound I could use for a slide?" I mentioned as an afterthought.

"We're quite busy planting right now," Richard replied, frowning a little.

Right then, Sharon walked in, followed by Patrick with another tray of tea.

"Oh, Richard," Sharon said, "can you send a couple of your guys up to fix Lauren's window boxes?" Richard turned to frown at her. "Hmmm, what we need is a nice chocolate cake for this afternoon," Sharon went on without pausing, eyeing the tea tray in an effort to make everything—well, as it should be. We all traipsed back into the kitchen to rifle through the pantry, checking for ingredients; Richard liked the idea of a chocolate cake too. There was no flour or cocoa powder. I suggested that we make up the brownie mix I had brought back with me from America, but Richard laughed and said he hadn't seen eggs for weeks. Sharon shifted sticky canisters around, billowing little clouds of dust, looking for something we could have right then. "Lucy," she called, " are there any biscuits in here?" Lucy came quickly and shifted canisters around too, billowing up more dust, wanting to be helpful. "God, this place is a mess," Sharon finally said, exasperated.

We decided to at least have tea outside, where, in an effort to lure away the flies, Richard had hung plastic bags full of soupy, rotting *kapenta* from the trees. The stench of the fermenting fish and decomposing cow manure from the too-close corral assaulted our sweaty faces with every slight shift in the breeze. Before long, we predictably got up and moved the tray inside.

It was remarkable how fast our days on Semahwa slipped into languid fly-buzzing time. The telephone was broken. With no flour to make Play-Doh and no blocks to build with, eventually I dug out buckets and jars and turned on the hose outside. At first, when Richard came up from the fields for tea, he seemed happy to see the children splashing and having fun; after a day or two, he reminded me it was the dry season and reckless to waste water.

Sharon and I slouched on the sofa, trying to think of new ways to entertain Luke and the other children while Lucy prepared us simple meals that usually consisted of a small bowl of rice or cornmeal, a few dry pieces of some sort of meat, a little grated beetroot, and a few slices of green bell pepper—the only vegetables currently in the garden. Samantha, Claudia,

Hanna, and Niamh usually refused to touch any of it. In the beginning, I had resignedly brought the Cheerios to the table, but when Luke reached across, opening and closing his little hand as he cried, " 'Eerios, 'eerios," Richard stopped me from passing him any. "Luke's got to learn to eat what's in front of him," he told me. After that, Sharon and I made it clear to our children, through whispers and looks, that they had to eat their Cheerios in the kitchen and were only allowed to disappear from the table one at a time.

We took long naps during the heat of the day. I wandered through to the kitchen sometimes and asked Lucy when she thought Sandra might be coming, and she always smiled and said "Soon." When we reminded Richard about the playground or the window boxes, he always said "Tomorrow" or "Later," until Sharon gave up altogether, and I went to the compound to scrounge materials myself. Bernard, in the workshop, only had about five or six old tires too worn through for any other possible use, and he eventually parted with one long piece of precious nylon rope. First, I got Francis to climb the *masuku* tree and hang the tire swing, and then he partially buried the remainder of the tires in a kind of permanent obstacle course that I arranged. Richard and Luke were both excited and happy with our efforts, but I was a little disappointed, my playground not being quite what I had imagined.

One morning Richard arrived back at the house whooping and giggling, shouting for us all to come outside and look. We peered cautiously into the flatbed of his pickup and saw a large, brown, hairy bush pig surrounded by a seeping black pool of blood. Its lips had fallen back slackly to reveal two fat yellowed tusks. Alarmed, we retreated toward the kitchen door. Hopping up and down with excitement, Richard explained how difficult it was to shoot the bush pigs that guzzled his corn in densely planted fields. They had a proclivity to explode out from behind thick stalks to tear at your calves with their angry sharp teeth. Hearing this, the children were all terrified and ran inside to hide. Patrick and Francis were left to pull the immense dead pig off the back of the truck. They dropped it on the ground with a wet thud before dragging it closer to the kitchen, leaving a long, meandering brown smear on Lauren's small patch of yellow lawn. Hacking with dull knives, they carved the animal into bloody chunks and then wrapped the dismembered bits into odd pieces of grubby shopping bags prior to popping every last sinew into the freezer, where I knew it all waited, frosty fragments of colored plastic slipping off a still-snarling head, staring out through deadly white-glazed eyes.

Filled with a kind of restless energy, I decided to make my four-year-old Claudia's Zambian experience educational. Her preschool in Westport had a Unicef book entitled *Children Just Like Me*, and I encouraged her to make a similar kind of report, which would undoubtedly impress her teachers back home. I approached Lucy about finding children in the compound whom we could interview.

After a day or two, as I was keeping an eye on the children playing an elaborate game of lining up stones in the flatbed of Richard's old pickup, I noticed a black family in the distance straggling through the bush. I immediately grabbed the kids, my notebook, and yelled for Francis, the surprised gardener, to translate, all of us charging off through thorny grass to intercept the little group. The father was a stooped and ashy man dressed in a worn-thin dirty coat that hung loosely on his slight frame. His wife was wrapped and tied in stained cloth. He smiled toothlessly, while she wore a witless expression. With them were four children, all clothed in diaphanous fragments, snot encrusting their noses and flies milling around their eyes.

Ignoring their puzzled faces, I accosted them with chit-chatty questions in my school-teacher voice. To one little girl who looked about Claudia's age: "What's your favorite game? What's your favorite food? Uh, what's your least favorite food? My little girl doesn't like vegetables, right, honey?" I said, nodding enthusiastically at Claudia, encouraging her to join in, teaching her to be assertive and confident. I turned my attention quickly back to the young black girl, wanting to maintain the momentum, the enthusiasm, and make it fun for everyone, "And what do you want to be when you grow up?" I asked her cheerfully.

Francis, who was translating, spoke slowly, studying his bare feet in the dirt. The little girl he was addressing appeared nervous and glanced anxiously at her parents. Her father was staring at me, half smiling, willing to please but unable to understand what I wanted.

"Francis, are these the people Lucy arranged for me to talk to?" I finally asked impatiently. Francis shrugged. He didn't know anything about interviewing children or impressing teachers in Westport. This family did not work on the farm, he explained to me. They were merely cutting through, on the way from somewhere to somewhere else. Everyone stood watching me expectantly. "Tell them it's a mistake," I sheepishly instructed Francis, who translated into Tonga, and the little family picked up their heavy bundles again and said, "Eh, eh," as if *mazungu* mistakes were not at all uncommon.

Sharon and I were a little tired of beets and green peppers and, certain that the meat Lucy was now preparing was that unappetizing bush pig, I asked Richard if I could pick some corn. "It's pretty tough this time of year," Richard replied dubiously, but I was insistent, so he shrugged and drove Lucy and me down to the field, had a quick word with an old man who emerged from the bushes there—a guard, Richard explained—and then yelled, "I'll be back in twenty minutes. Make sure you try to find tender ones!"

Lucy walked ahead of me, directly into the tall maize. "Lucy," I called, trotting after her a little anxiously.

"You have to walk in there"—she pointed—"otherwise it's too tough," she called back.

Suddenly, tender corn did not feel like the priority. I watched Lucy's brightly printed *chitenge* flashing and turning before quickly disappearing into the tall swaying stalks. "Lucy!" I yelled, suddenly terrified by the ominous expanse of rustling corn, the wizened old man staring curiously at me, and the prospect of bush pigs tearing out and ripping off someone's calves. "Lucy!" I yelled a third time, louder and more insistently. "The corn on the edge of the road here is just fine." I was adamant, so she reappeared, a little disappointed, but didn't argue. We picked a few ears from the places I'd chosen and then sat down on the side of the road to wait for Richard. Later, when we ate that corn, it tasted like cement.

After about two and a half weeks, Sandra still hadn't arrived. It was unclear from Lucy exactly where she had to come from. "Far," was all Lucy said.

"Is there anyone else we can interview?" I asked. Lucy thought politely for a while and then shook her head. "No."

"No one from the compound?" I insisted. She thought again. "No."

Richard asked Sharon and me if we would watch Luke for a few days while he went fishing. A little apprehensive about being left on the farm alone, we were also aware of the strain Richard had been under lately and so wanted to give him an opportunity to relax. In preparation for his departure, he showed us how to use the farm radio and left us the keys to the pickup in case of an emergency. I'm not sure whether he was aware that neither of us could ever find our way back to the main Lusaka road, even if we needed to.

Sharon found the prospect of yet more lonely days on the farm a little daunting, so she used the radio to invite a few of the district wives over for Sunday lunch. There were, after all, lemons on the tree for the gin, two chickens in the freezer with the remains of the pig, and plenty of rice. Although Lucy had the day off, we were sure we could rustle up a semblance of salad from the vegetable garden. There were a few tins of canned peaches for dessert. Sharon set about digging in the linen cupboard for clean napkins and place mats and began to wonder if there were any roses blooming in the garden that could be used for a table arrangement.

When Caroline, our first guest, arrived that Sunday morning, she got out of her jeep and casually asked if we knew that the farm was on fire. The flames were already quite close to the compound, she added, rather unperturbed, opening her trunk to take out the flowers she had brought for Lauren's grave.

"Fire?" Sharon asked disbelievingly. I was too dumbfounded to say a word. But Caroline didn't seem concerned. She calmly suggested that we find some of Richard's laborers to fight it—although, she added, it *was* Sunday and most of them had the day off. They would probably be playing soccer on the field near Popota, she offered. "I think I know where that is," Sharon said, running for the truck keys as I hurried after her. When she turned and saw my face, she reassured me, "Look, I'll put Niamh down for her nap and then you won't have so many to cope with," before she popped Niamh in the bedroom and closed the door.

"But Niamh will never sleep now, it's only eleven o'clock in the morning," I yelled after the pickup as it pulled away.

Niamh immediately howled and pounded on the door. Samantha and Luke, nervous of the stranger and the commotion, both tugged at my T-shirt: *Uppy, uppy, uppy!* Claudia and Hanna followed me around. "I want my mummy," Hanna whined in flat words she could barely squeeze around her firmly plugged-in thumb. The chickens remained on the table, the rice in the canister, and the table not yet laid. Another lady arrived. Niamh screamed and pounded harder.

I walked outside anxiously and sniffed. I thought I could

see smoke, but I wasn't certain; besides, African air is always burnt. I consoled myself that the ladies arriving for lunch seemed reasonably calm and we could leave quickly in their vehicles if it suddenly came to that.

The women poured themselves gin and tonics and started quietly to prepare lunch while Penny, who had been Lauren's closest friend in Choma, drove off to find Sharon. After an hour or so of unrelenting screaming from the bedroom, Corné, one of my guests, quietly retrieved a red and swollen-eyed Niamh, who gasped and shuddered in her arms, her sobs noisily settling into hiccups as she sucked hard on her knuckles and held the stranger tightly. I picked quietly at the meal my guests had produced without remembering to thank them.

When Sharon came back hours later, eyes wide and face smudged with soot, she grabbed a cold Coke from the refrigerator and gulped it down, explaining, between breaths, that when she had at first stopped in the compound, trying to get clear directions to the Popota field, the women sitting there straight-legged, in scraps of shade, had been evasive and uncooperative.

"It's Sunday," one woman had said, her chin jutting, squinting up at Sharon in the sun. The other women bent their heads and tittered in Tonga from behind cupped hands.

"But the fire is close to your house!"

"Eh, eh." The women clicked their tongues and shook their heads and looked meaningfully at one another. "It is not my house," the same woman said boldly, and the other ladies all tittered again.

Exasperated, and without clear directions, Sharon drove twisting dirt tracks in search of the workers' field. Eventually she found it: a barren patch of brown earth with listing goal posts perched tentatively at either end. Shirtless men in ragged pants, glistening with sweat and laughing loudly with glazed and bloodshot eyes, were squatting under trees and lounging on rocks drinking African beer. Some were running quite energetically on the baking field but others had draped heavy arms around each other, holding themselves up. They laughed uproariously when they saw Sharon, a confused *mazungu* standing next to her pickup. "Which are the Semahwa workers?" Sharon asked. In response, a man leaned too close to her, scornfully slurring words she didn't understand. "It's an emergency," she explained politely to someone else, who again chuckled and shook his head, shouting something to his friends, and they all roared to the sky and then bent double, slapping their thighs.

Luckily, Sharon told us, Penny arrived just then. She got out quickly, marched over, and said something tight-lipped in Tonga, which roused a few sniggers but left the glossy red-eyed men less confident. Penny raised her voice and repeated herself more slowly, and only then did four or five of the men sigh and follow her on resigned, rubbery legs.

"It was so hot," Sharon remembered, as she explained how she had worked downwind, frantically beating at embers. Men fumbled and staggered, she said, dropping buckets and tools while the driver of the tractor, which dragged yards of water-soaked burlap over the brittle yet unburned grass, kept driving into trees, wobbling dangerously on impact, then blinking in blurry surprise until he suddenly remembered where he was.

In the middle of this, Richard unexpectedly emerged in a borrowed vehicle. He slammed the car door, strode over to the tractor, and in one motion pulled the unsteady driver off his seat, punching him hard to the ground. Richard's voice was loud, his orders bellowing through scorching air. The laborers suddenly moved faster, ran straighter.

Sharon and I were indignant that Richard had hit the tractor driver, Sharon confiding to me that the trees he had driven into were not very big, just saplings really. But Richard remained unapologetic. When he walked into the farmhouse living room that evening, after the ladies had all gone home and Sharon's children had stopped sniffling on her lap, he cracked open a cold beer, turned on the TV, and put his feet up.

"Sharon said you hit the tractor driver."

"He was driving my tractor drunk." Sharon and I glanced at each other.

"Quite a fire, that," I said conversationally, looking for a compliment. Or a thank-you.

"They're common this time of year." Another long pause.

"We were pretty worried it would reach the compound."

"The breaks would've taken care of it," he said. All of us now concentrated on the TV.

"We weren't expecting you home so soon," I said.

"There were no fish," Richard replied. "And the mosquitoes were driving me crazy."

AS WE CONTINUED TO WAIT FOR SANDRA, I IMAGINED WHAT SHE would be like. San-dra. I knew she would be perfect. Even her name sounded—well, like Mary Poppins. Every day, I eagerly asked Lucy if she had heard from Sandra. Every day, Lucy calmly answered, "She is coming."

Sandra finally arrived just a week or so before I was due to return to Connecticut. She greeted me in halting English, cautiously stepping into the cool of the farmhouse as if she might break something. She cooed admiringly at the refrigerator and pulled and pushed the drawers of Luke's bureau, savoring its smoothness and nodding at the roundness of the handles. I offered her some tea, so we could talk, and she poured the entire contents of the sugar bowl into her cup and then licked at the hot paste, too entranced to answer my questions. Before she left, she asked whether she could take Luke's used but not-too-peed-on American disposable diapers for her own children.

Sandra's first afternoon at work, I watched from the window as she flirted with Francis, grinning at him with purple teeth from too many mulberries off the tree, while Luke whimpered, confused and lost, some distance from her. I ran outside to scoop him up, blinking back hurt and tears, before explaining to Sandra that she needed to *interact* with Luke. I carried out his few books and puzzles and gesticulated at them, Sandra smiling and nodding. Luke had been cleaned and fed; Sandra, who was happy to have a job, considered her work done. She hadn't understood anything I said.

"Sandra's hopeless," Sharon finally admitted one afternoon. I had to agree, panicked at the prospect of having to find a replacement when we had so little time.

I started to observe Luke with the two gardeners, Francis and Robson, one gardener mowing, the other holding the electric cable with Luke, making sure he stayed out of the way. I saw how Luke watered the vegetables with one of them, washed the pickup with the other, squatting down close to both of them while they paused for their morning tea, everyone appearing to enjoy both the talking and the silences.

"I've seen Francis in the compound with his own child," Richard said, a little uncertainly, looking over my shoulder. "He holds his son's hand and stops when he stops, and talks to him softly," he went on, waiting for my response. I wasn't sure what to think. Could Francis read Luke stories? What about toilet training? Francis stared out from wary eyes that hovered above three pale tribal scars running down each cheek. Could he put a Band-Aid on a scraped knee? Did he bend to tie shoes? None of my images of nurture included anything like Francis.

"How about we do this temporarily," Sharon said, as she got out a pen and her diary and began to scribble a schedule. "Patrick can stay on early morning duty. Lucy can do bath times and supper. Then we'll get Francis and Robson. . . ." Her pen darted as she wrote in lunchtimes, teatimes, and afternoons off.

"Well, let's try it," I said uncertainly, knowing that we had no other choice.

Sharon left Zambia a few days before I did. I used the extra time to stack and restack my laminated notes on child rearing in Richard's bathroom and to tape inspirational messages, like REMEMBER TO BREATHE, all over the house. I noted what was missing from the first-aid kit and pestered Richard to take out a medical insurance policy that would airlift both him and Luke out of Zambia in case of an emergency.

The psychologists I had spoken to in America had suggested I try to talk to Luke about Lauren, to keep her memory an easy open subject, so I carried Samantha and Luke out to Lauren's grave. There they both immediately clambered up that tall high mound of stony gravel and sat down happily. "Your mummy died, Lukie. Do you miss her?" was all I managed to say before sobbing. Luke and Samantha both frowned at me, completely mystified.

"No throwing stones," Luke said, picking up a small pebble, aiming it at Samantha, and checking with me to see if the rule might have changed. Helplessly, I realized that I couldn't even explain what *dead* was, so when I got back to the house I told Francis that the next time he found a dead bird or mouse in the garden he should please dig a grave and hold a little burial for Luke's benefit. Francis nodded at me dubiously, probably convinced I was near certifiable by now.

The day I was to leave, Richard asked whether I minded getting a lift back to Victoria Falls with some farmers who were driving there anyway. When we got to their house, the flatbed of their pickup was already packed with towering sacks of *kapenta*. Vicious dogs ran up and down the fence barking, and Richard warned Lucy to stay in the car.

I asked about the concrete slab outside the kitchen door, and Richard said casually, "For carcasses." He tied my suitcase on the very tippy-top of the *kapenta* while I distractedly wondered if it could possibly stay there for the hours it would take to get to the airport.

"Thank you," Richard said, kicking the ground bashfully. "You and Sharon made such a difference. It was"—his voice became softer and he finished quietly—"so difficult until you got here."

I held on to Luke tightly, aware of his light breath on my neck and the way he absently twirled my hair. He trusted me by then. I had used all the textbook mothering skills I had learned: reading to him and giggling with him at bedtimes, pushing him high on his new tire swing, and holding him tightly when he cried.

But who was going to do that now? There was an unbearable tightness in my throat as I felt his life shudder back into terrifying, unmothered emptiness.

"I'm coming back in about six weeks," I blurted.

"You are?" Richard replied. He sounded pleasantly surprised. "But don't you have anything to do in America?" he added.

I squeezed Luke hard, then handed him quickly back to Lucy.

"Wendy! Wendy!" he cried, reaching out his arms as I walked away and climbed into the truck. Lucy jiggled him gently on her lap, softly shushing him.

I sobbed as we pulled away. Claudia gently stroked my thigh and murmured, "It's OK, Mommy, it's OK, Mommy," and when I stared down into her four-year-old face, I suddenly realized that this was the first time I'd really looked at her in over a month. Her eyes were darker brown and more serious than I'd remembered. Her lips trembled anxiously, and I noticed she had put her small arm protectively around Samantha's shoulders, who was watching me nervously too. "It's OK, Mommy," Claudia whispered again soothingly, mothering me. "We're going home."

14

When I returned to Zambia in early December of that year, the whole country was desperate for rain. This feverish waiting-for-rain is an annual rite in southern Africa. I knew it well from my childhood when, from October on, the perimeters of lush city suburbs with their boreholes and sprinklers suddenly shrunk to insignificance, while miles of parched land stretching out into the horizon seemed to rise up gasping as though the African continent itself was on the verge of death. Sometimes dry months rolled into January. Sometimes the rain never came at all.

In Zambia for just ten days this time, I left Claudia and Sebastian with Mickey and took only Samantha with me. Sharon met us at Victoria Falls again with Hanna and Niamh, and we drove up to the farm—searing air assaulting us through the open pickup windows, the earth outside so dry it was almost painful to watch.

As we clattered our bags into the barely lit kitchen, I heard Lucy's voice from the bedroom at the end of the long hall, urging Luke to hurry. After a few moments, they both appeared; Luke freshly bathed and pink-cheeked, holding Lucy's hand. He was a little taller, and his hair had grown. I walked toward them and, careful not to overwhelm him, I hugged Lucy first before kneeling down to say hi to Luke. He twisted away coyly, and I stood up again, ready to give him time.

The drapes and swags Sharon had hung so carefully on the last trip were thoroughly caked in red dust; I resignedly made a mental note to put them away. I noticed that Patrick had been carefully propagating Lauren's African violets on a sunny shelf in the hall, the way Gail used to at Bien Donné. He must have watched Lauren diligently line up rows of glass jars, each with a fuzzy violet leaf poked through a piece of plastic secured with an elastic band, a forest of stems all dangling into their private pond of murky water. For some reason I found those stems oddly comforting.

As I was unpacking in the dim light, adjusting to the infinite quiet surrounding me, Patrick knocked softly. He handed me an empty tube of toothpaste that I had left in the bathroom weeks before, eagerly showing me that it had a few more squeezes. I thanked him. I had also left something else behind, he added, encouraged. He pushed past me and pointed to my deodorant lid, untouched after weeks on the bureau. I smiled, thanking him again.

I walked through to the living room with a little present for Luke, luring him nearer, wanting him to be close to me again. "What have you been doing, sweet pea?" I said, and I stroked his back while he plucked at the colored ribbons on his gift. Within moments, he had taken the bait, climbing onto my lap and cuddling down safe and warm again.

Aware we had limited time, Sharon buzzed around like a mosquito. Should we pull up the pennyroyal from under the roses? Where were the silver napkin rings Uncle Alastair gave Lauren for her wedding? How old is this rice? What are we going to do about Lauren's clothes?

"Leave them alone," Richard said, pulling his hat down low over his eyes as he walked away. Lauren's scrunchies were still on the bedpost, her makeup on the dresser, her robe hanging behind the bedroom door. And that was just the beginning. Almost every closet in the house was jammed with Lauren's old shoes, handbags, and other paraphernalia.

"You can't just leave all this stuff lying around forever," I called to Richard, trying to sound a little gentler than Sharon. Because I sensed I was gaining ground, I continued. "How about we just do the closet in the spare room? I know Lauren never wore any of those old outfits."

"You can clear it out if everything leaves the country," he finally said. "I don't want to see any of it in the compound. And don't touch anything in my room," he added over his shoulder. We said, "Yes, yes," and waited for him to leave.

Sharon and I started going through Lauren's clothes, aghast

at the amount of junk she had accumulated. "Oh my God, look at this," I squealed, holding up an old black satin bustier that laced down the front.

"And this!" Sharon declared, gleefully tugging out a pair of worn leopard-print leggings. "Lol, did you wear them together?" She shrieked, laughing hysterically.

"Wait, wait!" I chuckled, reaching far into the back, grabbing a once-green piece of brittle Lycra. "This was *your* Kariba bikini from about twenty years ago. Groovy, hey?" I teased Sharon. Amazed, we continued to pull out armfuls of tumbled clothes: wide gypsy skirts, prim dresses with Peter Pan collars, sexy jeans, fake tweed jackets, disintegrating leather coats, all the pastel polyester outfits I'd once sent home from New York.

Remember, remember, remember? we roared, plucking at each stale old memory, stopping at a soft black beret that Lauren had taken with her to England. I plonked it on my head. "Remember this?" I asked more quietly. We both remembered how Lauren had worn it, so vulnerable, trying desperately to appear sophisticated. I took it off and smelled it, hungry for the scent of her.

"Let me try," Sharon said, snatching it from me as I moved on to sniff the other clothes piled high on the bed, ferreting out little pieces of Lauren to hold.

Sharon and I stuffed it all into bags, dusted our hands, and congratulated ourselves on a job well done. I knew that no one within a hundred-mile radius of Westport was likely to want any of it, so I planned to give it away at the airport in spite of what Richard had said. Within seconds I'd have a noisy crowd all around me, clucking and arguing, happily waving green and pink and lilac polyester, like flags.

One early evening, we found Richard sitting outside on the scraggly front lawn staring wistfully at the sky. Sharon and I brought him a cold beer and a bag of stale potato chips and took seats next to him, ignoring the flies, breathing out when the wind blew the scent of rotting *kapenta* in our direction. The three of us were half talking and half watching his rib-thin cattle pathetically nose for nonexistent blades of grass in the dry corral when I noticed a man, quiet and unthreatening, about fifty yards away, holding a large rifle with a thick frayed strap.

Uncomfortable with the subtleties in Zambia, and never sure of proper cause for alarm, I said, "Richard, there's a man over there with a gun."

Richard glanced up. "Oh, that's Moses, my game guard."

"You have game?" I asked, surprised.

Smiling for the first time in days, Richard replied, "No, people around here get pretty desperate for food. One dry season a few starving guys opened the gates of my dam to drain off the remaining shallow water so they could snatch at the muddy fish left at the bottom. Moses fends them off."

"And he needs a gun that size?"

"Some poachers have automatic weapons," Richard said, laughing. "But most of these poor buggers are just hungry," he went on. "A couple of weeks ago I chased this bloke down for trapping guinea fowl on the farm, but then I discovered that

all he had in his hut was honey and a few gaunt children."
Richard shook his head, and then added, "I let him go."

I glanced over to where Moses waited for Richard to take
the gun for safekeeping overnight. I wanted to take a photo of
this gentle-looking man with the vengeful-looking weapon and
Richard said it was OK to ask.

Walking up to him, I showed Moses my camera and he
smiled, cautiously nodding his assent. I posed him against the
garage wall, a black man against a white wall, and I peered
through my viewfinder. Moses was short and wearing heavy
boots, a once-white too-big shirt, and ragged pants with holes
in the knees. His skin was very dark and scarred. I could smell
his human odor of sweat and smoke.

But there was something missing. I wanted to capture an
image of Moses' person and there was nothing coming from
his eyes. I put my camera down and began to ask him questions
about his family, his day, trying to spark an emotion, yet Moses
remained tense and passive, a guarded blank, ready to respond
to any unintelligible or irrational thing I might require of him.
There was an ancient cookbook on Lauren's shelf that had been
printed for early white settlers in Kenya with a translated list
of apparently useful phrases: Fetch the washing, Bring the
dinner, Make the beds, Do the dishes. I realized there were no
questions. Generations later white women raised in Africa still
didn't ask questions. Had Moses ever had a *mazungu* interested
in him beyond what she wanted?

I knew what it was to let go of your spirit, to offer empty
guarded eyes. I stared hard at Moses and recognized power-
lessness. I knew it well.

. . .

WE HAD BEEN IN ZAMBIA FOR FIVE DAYS WHEN SHARON NOTICED that Chunky, the muscular, brown-black Rottweiller with rusty markings on his face and feet, was sick. Lauren had loved Chunky. On their long walks across the farm, Chunky barked away impudent baboons and fat lazy snakes resting in her path. When the squatters moved onto Semahwa, Chunky trotted protectively next to her. He lay at her feet while she stirred dinner in the dim kitchen light and kept her company when Richard was away hunting or fishing. Luke learned to stand, pulling himself up by Chunky's thick fur.

Now Chunky lay thin and listless next to his bowl of untouched food on the peeling black-and-white checkerboard kitchen floor.

"Richard." Sharon accosted him as he walked in from the scorched fields. "Chunky's sick," she announced, her hands on her hips.

" I know."

"I think you should take him to the vet."

"Do you know how far away the vet is?"

"We'll drive him."

"I can't spare the fuel," Richard replied. He found whatever it was he'd come back to the house for and was off again.

Sharon shouted over him as he kick-started his motorbike. "Well, you can't let him die!" Richard didn't answer.

Sharon became fixated on Chunky, as if she had suddenly decided that not one more heart was going to stop. Sitting on the floor with the dog's head in her lap, she would stroke him

and nurse him, rolling up slippery morsels of *sadza*, corn porridge, and gravy to push between Chunky's feeble lips. When
Richard came anywhere near the house, Sharon followed him,
her arms crossed—"Richard, Richard, Richard"—less like a mosquito now, more like an electric drill. Something heavy in
Richard started to swing shut.

Sharon paced and complained. She radioed neighbors who
commiserated and agreed: yes, Richard could be difficult. But
not one offered to drive Chunky to the vet. Rummaging
through the house, Sharon found old blankets and blocks of
ice before finally coming across Richard's medical supplies.
Never mind that the antibioics had been prescribed for adult
humans. After guessing Chunky's weight, she ground three
tablets up into some *sadza* and fed the dog lovingly by hand.

"Sharon!" Richard yelled from the farm office, marching
into the kitchen. "Where are the rest of these tablets?" he demanded, shaking the empty bottle in her face.

"I left the whole container on the desk," she replied
meekly, suddenly worried.

"Did you touch this?" Richard shouted at Luke.

"I ate it," Luke whimpered, confused. Richard grabbed him
quickly, rushed him to the toilet, and forced thick fingers
down his throat. Screaming and kicking, Luke managed only
bile, tears dribbling off his lips. Richard tried again, pushing
his fingers down farther, leaving Luke gagging and choking,
unable to breathe.

He put Luke down and frantically radioed Caroline:
"Chenga, Chenga—Chenga, Chenga from Semahwa," he

begged, and when we finally heard Caroline's voice pick up on the other end, Richard blurted details of the crisis.

"He'll probably just end up with a bad case of the runs," Caroline's voice crackled uncertainly, "but it really depends on how many he took." We didn't know. "Well, if he took a lot, it is possible that his throat will swell closed," she explained carefully, "but if that happens, it will happen within the next half hour. You'd never make it to the clinic in time, Richard. Over."

Richard slid down the office wall, his head in his hands. I picked up Luke, now terrified, and held him close. Sharon was crying too. "I'm so sorry, Richard, I'm so sorry."

We waited like that for ten, fifteen, twenty minutes. I sang Luke little songs, told him stories, anything to keep him very still. The other children watched from the door. Twenty-five, thirty minutes. Luke was quite chatty by then, but I was still holding him firmly.

"A kudu got stuck," he offered, conversationally.

"A kudu?" A kudu is a large big-horned antelope.

"In the fence," he told me. "The boys got it." Luke frowned at me, crossing and uncrossing his ankles with sudden energy, remembering the noise and the confusion. I pressed his body still. Thirty-five, forty minutes.

"They ate it," he said, an abrupt finish to his story.

A little distant and preoccupied before, now Richard shut down completely. For days later, he came in from the fields, walked right past us without saying a word, and turned on the TV. He ate without calling us to join him. As if we weren't there at all, he went about his life, cutting up Luke's toast, pouring his tea, instructing Lucy or Francis about his naps, making it very clear that Luke was his child, not ours.

Perhaps a day or two afterward, Chunky died. Francis and Robson dug a deep hole near Lauren's old chicken coop, and we buried him there. Luke abruptly learned what dead was, as I'd wanted him to.

Feeling listless, I wandered the farmhouse, looking for little chores, passing and repassing Patrick, who would flash quick gap-toothed smiles in my direction and then look down again quickly, as is polite in Africa.

I followed Patrick out to the washing line to help with a big basket of laundry and asked him how he had been since the last time I was in Zambia. Eager to respond, he wanted to know whether I knew he was the religious leader in the compound. Had I noticed the church he was building? I had to confess, sheepishly, that I hadn't (although when he showed the partially built structure to me later it was so overgrown with grass and scrub I believe it was forgivable to have missed it). Patrick chatted away, telling me he was working on his O levels, the British-administered high school examination. It was difficult, he said, because his wife was epileptic and needed medication, and the textbooks were expensive. On top of that were the examination fees, he added sadly. Sometimes, he said, he saved for the books, and then the examination fees, only to discover that the books he bought years before had gone out of date. We paused together in the sun, as is polite in Africa.

The time Sharon and I had left was spent in the cool shade at Lauren's grave while the children chased lizards, collected msasa pods, or lay splayed out on the hot sand, tickling for ant lions. We found railway sleepers and cinder blocks to make a bench. We hauled out the old birdbath that lay rusting and forgotten next to the house and dragged pots of geraniums from the veranda, arranging them artistically with twisted bits of wood. The white bougainvillea we planted was frugally watered with precious drops of water.

One afternoon, for something to do, I decided to take some photographs and walked with Lucy down to the compound while the children were all napping. Birds perched quietly, as if momentarily stunned by the heat. Our feet crunched the sand together, echoing in companionable silence.

"Do you think Luke is OK?" I asked Lucy, after a while.

"He is OK."

"Does he miss his mummy?"

"Yes, he misses her."

"But he is OK though, right? Do you think he will be OK?"

She stopped and smiled at me. "Yes, he will be OK."

We walked on together. I licked the dry dust coating the inside of my mouth. Lucy paused every so often, bending at the waist, to pick up *masukus*, a bitter bush fruit, sucking on them as we walked, spitting the pit discreetly into her palm before tossing it into the long crackling grass.

When we reached the compound people emerged from their huts, curious and eager to get in front of my camera. Some children cried if I came too close; others darted and danced, shaking their skinny hips. Even the men, curious, came out of the workshop, and when they saw what was going on, they strutted and posed, lifting big tractor tires, flexing their muscles. We communicated in sign language, since most of them didn't speak English and I spoke no Tonga. "Why are so many of these kids out of school?" I asked Lucy.

"They have no money for uniforms or fees," she said simply, smiling at the commotion, still sucking on her handful of *masukus*.

"Where is it?"

"Maybe ten kilometers."

"How do kids get there?"

"They walk."

I started to look at Lucy and to watch the way she moved, like someone who was confident of the way her world turned. One morning we had sat together on the warm kitchen step after clearing away breakfast dishes, and she told me she had once been married to a Zimbabwean who, like Lauren, was killed in a car accident. Rich enough to own a car, he had given Lucy a good life alongside his. When he died, she was left with two small boys and so had to find work in the fields of Richard's farm. "It was a struggle," she said simply, and we sat silently together for a while, thinking.

"What makes you happy, Lucy?" I asked her, really wanting to know. First she smiled, and after a moment passed, she said, "My children." We both looked into each other's eyes and laughed from a place deep down where our motherhood lay.

In that season after Lauren died, the rain finally came one late afternoon, heralded by cool low winds, carried in on massive fat clouds that staggered dark and drunken, suddenly unable to contain themselves, exploding water onto the parched ground. Exhilarated, Sharon, Richard, and I jumped into the pickup, faces pressed up to the wipers, trying to see past the sheets of water on the windscreen, eventually putting our heads out of the windows. We were laughingly drenched, greedy to taste the water falling, to see the streams and rivulets tearing at the earth around the young crops, gouging deeper gullies into the road, breathing in beginnings.

When we got back to the house, the fragile electrical system had been knocked out, as it always is in a storm. We groped for candles, held the kids tightly, and felt the thunder reverberate. Perched in front of a window, we watched the black sky as lightning ripped in the dark. It was hard not to smile, deafened by pounding rain, feeling so close to the earth.

Southern Africa changes quickly after the first heavy rains. Dust is washed out of the air, making the sky look cleaner and brighter. The earth pushes up pale green shoots against the harsh oranges and browns of before. The land smells rich and promising.

For the next day or two the atmosphere on the farm was more buoyant, the voices in the compound more hopeful. I saw Moses again, after the tractor had just pulled away. He came walking up the road in thick boots, tired after a night's patrol, with his gun in one hand and an incongruous large white mushroom, like a small parasol, in the other. I had tasted those huge mushrooms before, peculiar delicacies that appear in the bush only after the first heavy rains. Moses saw me, held up his mushroom like a toast, and smiled. I understood. A trophy. A release and a fresh start. I smiled back. The spark in his eyes was a little brighter. Marginally closer. A fragile thread connected us.

Moses.

epilogue

At any given moment, I can tell you how long Lauren has been gone. It's not just because of the singsong symmetry to her life—born '66, buried '99, just thirty-three when she died—but because I have a kind of stopwatch in my head, like the crocodile that swallowed Captain Hook's hand, and I tick, forever aware of exactly how long Luke has been without his mother.

He is seven and a half now, and I continue to visit him often since Lauren's death. Richard no longer picks me up on the Zimbabwean side of the falls; one symptom of the region's political troubles is the police there, who have fallen into galloping free-for-all lawlessness, demanding bribes and fining vehicles in American dollars for arbitrary offenses like having a cracked wing mirror or parking with a tire on the line demarcating individual spots.

Because Sharon knows someone in the travel business, she has me escorted from Victoria Falls in a sticky dilapidated tour bus. The formerly quiet border post has changed a lot. It's choked with people blocking the road, noisily arguing or conducting secret business with furtive glances, money slipping from palm to palm as bundles are wrapped and unwrapped. Most years, there are rusty food-aid trucks stretched in a line across the bridge, smelling of heat, spewing black clouds, loaded with corn covered by dirty canvas and thick thorn branches, deterrents to hungry people and baboons. The tour-bus drivers invariably manage to negotiate all this as I wait in the van while they take care of customs and immigration be-fore eventually dropping me off at the Waterfront, a backpack-ers' lodge on the Zambezi where Richard waits. I always make sure to give those drivers a hefty tip; I depend on them to get me back.

Luke goes to school on a farm over an hour away from Semahwa that can accommodate fifteen or so local kids. Richard drops him off there on Monday mornings, collecting him again late on Friday afternoons. Although Semahwa does have a phone line that I know from experience works if some-one climbs up the tall gum pole to wiggle the cables, Richard seldom calls me. I am the one who spends the long hours every weekend dialing and redialing, hoping the telephone wires are lying just so, hoping to catch Luke for a few broken minutes.

Choma has an internet café now, although of course it's hardly a café, and the internet part of it seldom works, yet still Richard has used the place to contact me. Once I received an ecstatic run-on sentence about his hunt for a crazed and wounded buffalo that had stumbled onto the farm. Another message—with the subject line EMERGENCY! EMERGENCY!—was a request for a particular part for his gun.

I actually hadn't received an e-mail from Richard for a few years when I checked my in-box this past spring and found a message announcing his imminent arrival in America with Vicki, a new girlfriend, and Luke.

Knowing from experience how confusing phone cards, area codes, limos, and taxi lines could be, I arrived an hour early to wait for them at JFK. Richard was easy to spot as they came through customs, his deep tan shocking in New York's post-winter pastiness. Vicki, a white woman who had grown up on a farm close to Richard's in Zambia, smiled at me uneasily. Luke, in too-short hand-me-down jeans that I recognized from a package I had sent to Zambia years before, held his father's hand. I ran to greet them. "I'm so happy to see you," I said and knelt to hug Luke tightly. He stiffened a little, not having had one of my bear hugs for a while, and when I grabbed his hand, he turned apprehensively to check that Richard was behind us. Luke stumbled a little in his eagerness to stay very close as Richard, Vicki, and I all chatted about the flight, but I felt him freeze as the automatic doors ahead of us abruptly whooshed open. "Come on," I said, tugging Luke gently. Ducking, he ran through, pulling me by the arm into the chilly spring air.

My children were eager to impress Luke with the wonders of America, taking delight in explaining everything the country had to offer, from the miracle of Pop Tarts to the magic of dialing 911. They tried to drag him outside in the mornings to show off a real yellow school bus—impressive, flashy, and brake-squealing—but he pulled his hand away, wordlessly shaking his head, preferring to watch it all from the safety of the window.

With my kids in school, I spent the first day just driving Richard, Luke, and Vicki around Westport—to the beach, for a walk down our quaint Main Street. "How many people live in these houses?" Vicki wondered, staring out of the window at the vast facades blurring as we drove by.

"They're single-family homes," I muttered.

"Why do you need so many wires?" Luke asked, looking up at wrist-thick cables that draped back and forth in heavy swags supported by tired utility poles.

"Well, we have lots of—you know, stuff," I informed him.

I knew that salmon would be a treat for dinner, so we stopped to pick up a few fillets on the way home, and Richard murmured to Vicki, handing her the bag of fish as we left the store, "Just feel the quality of this plastic."

While Richard and Vicki went on a two-week motor tour of New England, Luke stayed with us. Barely out the door, Richard ran back. "If Luke starts vomiting or spikes a fever around 104 degrees, it'll be malaria," he quickly told me. "You know the symptoms, right?"

"Well . . . sort of," I replied, feeling decidedly rusty.

"If you don't treat it properly, malaria can kill him within forty-eight hours," Richard reminded me. "Whatever you do, don't take him to the doctor. They won't have a bloody clue how to handle malaria here and will probably put him into the hospital or something."

I nodded, agreeing with him. Hospital sounded about right.

"You'll have to use the antimalarial I left in the bathroom," he said.

"Are there directions on the box?" I asked, knowing full well that if Luke even *looked* like he had a fever, I'd be at the doctor's office in a second.

"I think so," he replied.

"Phone us often to let us know where you are," I called after him, as he hurried to the car. "Richard!" I shouted more loudly, making frantic dialing motions with my hand, to which he nodded vigorously, waving.

I was excited by the prospect of being alone with Luke. "We're going to Mystic Seaport," I announced that first morning. "It's an old whaling town here in Connecticut that they've kept exactly as it was more than a hundred years ago."

"Do we have enough fuel?" he asked.

"Yes," I said.

"What happens if children get carsick in America?"

"Plastic bags," I replied.

When we got there, Luke liked the old whaling ships well enough but wasn't impressed by animal-drawn carts, makeshift farm implements, or the old-fashioned schoolhouse where kids of all different ages once had their lessons just as they did at his school at home. After listening to a few cheery snippets of American history, Luke politely asked whether the longish grass at the edge of the historical settlement was a good place to take a pee.

"No, no," I said, quickly directing him to the bathroom, where I explained how the soap and towel dispenser worked and warned him not to touch the little blue disk in the urinal or be alarmed by the automatic flush. "Let's have lunch," I said afterward. We were in the cafeteria anyway, so we joined the line, where the woman in front of us noisily accused the teenager behind the cash register of touching her hot dog.

"I didn't touch it, ma'am," the youth replied.

"You did. I saw you," the woman insisted. Luke watched them both carefully.

"I didn't."

"You did."

The server sighed, calmly tipping the woman's entire tray of food into the trash.

"America is cooler than Zambia," Luke declared one morning as I was setting up a game of Monopoly.

"Why?" I asked, playing for time.

"It's got doorbells."

"Hmmm. . . ." I thought about it and then countered. "Zambia has the Victoria Falls, and that, young man, is one of the wonders of the world!" I poked him in the tummy to make my point.

"America's got yogurt drinks with pictures of the Incredibles," he said triumphantly, daring me to top that.

"Maybe one day you can come to school in America," I said, tracing patterns on his chest. "If you get good at Tonga or cricket or something, maybe you'll get a scholarship," I added.

"Will I be the only white boy in the whole of America who can speak Tonga?" he asked, suddenly interested.

"Yes," I said, without any hesitation at all.

Close to the end of his trip, Luke and I lay on the trampoline in the weak sun, waiting for the kids to come home from school. "What did my mummy look like?" Luke suddenly asked, shocking me. I felt my heart beat faster. Luke had seen pictures of Lauren. After she died, I had sent him dozens and dozens of laminated photos of her. I wanted Luke to drop them casually all over the house—down the back of the sofa, lost under pillows, tumbled with the linens.

I tried to keep my voice light. "Well," I began carefully, realizing that he didn't want to talk about her appearance, "She used to move her hands in this very beautiful way . . ."—I faltered a little—"like this." He was staring at me intently, his unblinking blue eyes rapt, so I sat up to demonstrate Lauren's hands more accurately. Growing frustrated that I wasn't getting it completely right, I laughed casually, not wanting to make him feel awkward.

"She also pulled this funny kind of face when she brushed her hair in the mirror," I went on. "It was kind of . . ." I found myself fumbling for those words too, so I pursed my lips slightly and fluffed up the hair at the crown of my head, to demonstrate.

As I glanced at him, he suddenly seemed smaller and peeled completely raw. I confronted a horrifying black loneliness in his heart at the very same moment I also understood the terrible impossibility of ever communicating his mother's spirit.

"And when she laughed, she threw her head back like this and went *ha, ha, ha*," I said, with forced gaiety, and Luke laughed so I did it again—"*ha, ha, ha*,"—and then I leaned down to kiss him, resting my lips in his hair, closing my eyes to regain my composure.

"And what happened when her car. . . ." He let the sentence wisp away.

"Crashed?" I said, tightly poised, and he nodded, staring at me.

"She was driving back from Zimbabwe when one of the wheels of the truck slipped off the road. She got frightened and turned the steering wheel too quickly, and the truck rolled over and over. She banged her head very hard. You and Lucy were in the truck, but Lucy covered you with a pillow and held on to you tightly so you weren't hurt."

"So it was the road's fault?"

"Yes. It was the road's fault," I said. There was a long silence and we looked at the sky together.

"Luke."

"Yes?"

"It's hard for me to explain exactly how beautiful and special your mummy was—on the inside, I mean. But there is one very, very important thing that I know she would really want you to hear." He stared at me. "She loved you so very much," I told him, and he nodded solemnly, and then I didn't want him to see me cry, so I turned away.

acknowledgments

I would like to thank my writer friends, Larry and Nancy Goldstone, who innocently suggested I pen an article about southern Africa and unwittingly unleashed a maelstrom. My appreciation for your guidance and support is incalculable.

To Jennifer Joel, my agent at ICM: Thank you for working so passionately on my behalf.

I am enormously grateful to Vanessa Mobley, my editor at Henry Holt and Company. With your sensitivity, astute insight, and painstaking attention to detail, you have taken my words and turned them into a book of which I am proud.

Sharon: Thank you for digging up old memories for me. I love you immeasurably.

Vonnie and Ian: I am so glad to be your sister. Your unfailing support has meant everything.

To my three children, Sebastian, Claudia, and Samantha, who have made the ultimate sacrifice in terms of their mother's time: You reeducate me every day about what love really is. Thank you.

And to Mickey, my beloved husband: Thank you for showing me the person I could become and then helping me get there. There are no words to express my gratitude for that.

illustration credits

Lauren and Luke
(Collection of G. Rossiter)

Lucy head shot
(Wendy Kann)

Wendy, Sharon, their mother
(Collection of W. Kann)

Three sisters as children
(Collection of W. Kann)

Wendy and Sharon in garden of house
(Collection of G. Rossiter)

Family portrait
(Photo by Ilio, collection of G. Rossiter)

Author's father with sable
(Collection of G. Rossiter)

Author's mother in wedding dress
(Collection of W. Kann)

Mickey with Soweto basketball team
(Collection of L. Frank)

Wendy and Mickey on their wedding way
(Collection of W. Kann)

Luke on the road
(Wendy Kann)

Moses with rifle, mushroom
(Wendy Kann)